Introduction to **UNIX System V**

by Robert A. Byers

Managing Editor: Robert Hoffman
Editor: Brenda Johnson
Text Design: Thomas Clark
Cover Design: D. A. Gray

Published by Ashton-Tate Publishing Group
10150 W. Jefferson Boulevard, Culver City, California 90230

ISBN 0-912677-29-5

ACKNOWLEDGEMENT

Writing this UNIX book has been fun. Several good people have contributed in a number of ways. Bill Jordan of Ashton-Tate talked me into writing it in the first place. Dennis Cohen at the Ashton-Tate Development Center and Scott D. Hansen of AT&T's Information Systems Laboratories both provided more than their fair share of technical help and guidance. Thanks, in particular, go to Jordan Brown of Ashton-Tate Development Center, who reviewed the manuscript.

Once you have all of the technical material together, it has to be translated into good English that also makes good sense. Robert Hoffman and Brenda Johnson of Ashton-Tate's Publications Group are the best and most patient editors.

I would also like to thank the Public Relations Department at AT&T Information Systems for their help in obtaining the photos appearing in this book.

Robert A. Byers

Table of Contents

CHAPTER ONE

WHAT IS UNIX?

UNIX is an operating system. An operating system is the necessary and fundamental part of your computer that transforms the hardware from pieces of metal and plastic into a computer, which you can use to solve business and scientific problems. You can use your computer profitably without knowing anything at all about its operating system. However, you can get much more value from your computer by learning to use at least some of the features of its operating system.

Most computer users don't actually choose an operating system. The operating system comes along with the purchase of a computer, like tires when you buy a car. Since you are reading this book, I will assume that you either have a computer with the UNIX operating system or you are contemplating the purchase of such a computer.

Computers with the UNIX operating system are usually designed to be used by more than one person at a time. Any computer that can be used by several people at the same time is called a *multi-user system*. A multi-user system is often chosen because the cost per user is less than the cost of providing each user with a personal computer. More importantly, however, a multi-user system allows its users to *share information*.

UNIX uses a technique known as *multi-tasking* in order to serve several users at a time. Each user is a separate *task* to the computer. The computer can perform only one

task at a time: To perform several tasks, it must switch back and forth between the various tasks. This switching takes place at such a high speed that each user is unaware that anyone else is using the computer. Multi-tasking also allows an individual user to perform two or more jobs at the same time.

In addition to being multi-user and multi-tasking, UNIX is *interactive*: The computer is capable of carrying on a dialogue with a user by means of the computer terminal or keyboard. These days, most computers operate this way. When UNIX was originally designed in 1969, most computers operated in a *batch* mode by reading punched cards.

Computers with UNIX are powerful—when judged by microcomputer standards. Figures 1-1 and 1-3 show two typical UNIX computers, AT&T's 3B2 and 3B5. A block diagram of a typical computer is shown as Figure 1-2. This diagram can be used to describe nearly any computer, from the smallest micro to the largest mainframe. The computer itself consists of the *central processing unit* (CPU), *main memory*, and *input/output* (I/O). The terminal, printer, modem, and the mass memory are called peripherals.

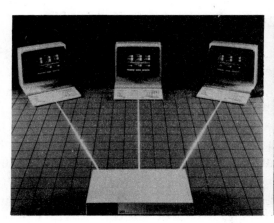

Figure 1-1 AT&T 3B2

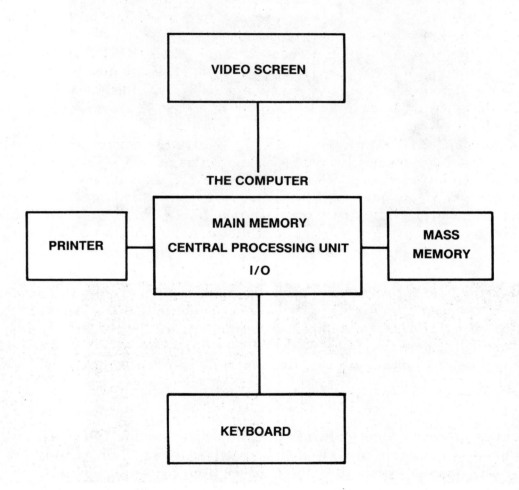

Figure 1-2 Block diagram of computer

CHAPTER ONE

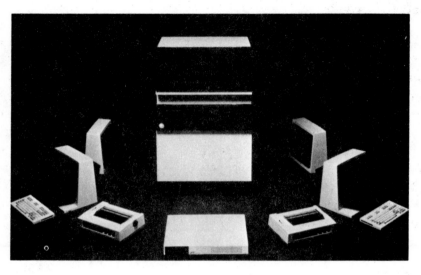

Figure 1-3 AT&T 3B5

Not long ago, most computers were located in computer centers and were tended by a professional priesthood. Most users were connected to the computer via the telephone system. Today, more and more computers are located in the offices they serve. These computers are often operated by the people who use them. Today's computers, therefore, must be powerful, simple, and reliable.

CPU

The central processing unit (CPU) is the part of the system that actually does the computing. Computers are often advertised as being 8-bit, 16-bit, or 32-bit machines. The number (8, 6, 32) is the *word size* used by the CPU. UNIX computers usually have 16-bit or 32-bit CPUs; their processors must be powerful because they are multi-tasking. One of the tasks of an operating system is managing the CPU and allocating its resources among the various tasks and users.

Bits, Bytes, and Words

Your computer stores information in units called *bytes*. A byte is the amount of memory required to store a character, such as an "," or an "A". Each byte is made up of eight bits. Each bit is like a tiny switch, which can be either on or off. The computer recognizes letters and other characters by the combined settings of these switches. There are a total of 256 possible settings for each byte; so, a byte can be used to represent up to 256 different things. (Most of us will never use a computer at the bit level; we use a computer at the byte level.)

A word consists of one or more bytes. In a 16-bit computer the word size is two bytes (16 bits). In a 32-bit computer the word size is four bytes (32 bits). Data is still usually stored in bytes, but more memory is generally available in computers with larger word sizes—which is important when a computer is to be shared by several users.

MAIN MEMORY

Main memory is used directly by the CPU. It consists of an enormous number of tiny electronic switches that store the programs and the data that the CPU is using at a particular time. There are two kinds of main memory: ROM and RAM. ROM stands for *Read Only Memory*. This memory permanently stores certain kinds of programs. Often, it is used to store a program that gets the computer going each time the computer is turned on: a *boot* program. RAM stands for *Random Access Memory*. Most of the computer's main memory is RAM. Random access memory is changeable, and it is the computer's working memory.

The amount of random access memory is usually expressed in kilobytes (Kbs). In computer systems, one kilobyte is 1024 bytes. UNIX computers require large amounts of main memory because the memory is shared by a number of users. UNIX must also allocate the computer's main memory between the various tasks and users.

INPUT/OUTPUT

Through Input/Output (I/O), the computer communicates with the outside world. The outside world consists of the terminals and printers connected to the

computer. Your computer will probably communicate with these devices by means of an RS-232C interface. This signal has become a standard interface between computers and peripheral devices. The operating system manages the communications between the computer and these devices.

Mass Memory

Mass memory consists of tape recorders and disk drives that permanently record information to be used by the computer. It can also augment the computer's main memory. Mass memory is significantly less expensive than main memory. It is also significantly (about a thousand times) slower.

Disk Drives A disk drive is like a magnetic phonograph. Information is stored on a rotating disk on magnetic tracks similar to the tracks on a phonograph record. A disk head moves in and out like the tone arm of a phonograph to read and write information on the disk. You store the programs, data, and text that you use on a day-to-day basis by means of the disk drive.

The disk drive is controlled by a disk controller that is connected to the I/O of the computer. The disk controller, under the direction of the CPU, controls the movement of the disk read/write head and places it at the correct position on the disk. The controller provides a path for the information flowing between the computer and the disk. It also keeps the CPU informed about conditions on the disk. The operating system is responsible for keeping a record of each item stored and its location on the disk. This record is called the *disk directory*.

Hard Disks On many of the newer computer systems, a hard disk is built into the computer and is located inside the computer cabinet. A computer with the UNIX operating system will probably have one or more hard disks. A hard disk is a machined metal platter which is coated with a magnetic material. There are two kinds of hard disks: fixed and removable. Fixed disk drives, called "Winchesters," are the least expensive and the most reliable. Removable disks are subject to damage primarily owing to handling. A typical hard disk system can store tens of millions of bytes (megabytes).

Floppy Disks Many computer systems have at least one floppy disk drive. A floppy disk is a mylar film coated with a magnetic substance. The mylar disk is packaged in a paper envelope to allow you to handle it easily. The paper envelope has slots cut into it that allow the disk to be mounted onto the disk drive hub and to provide the read/write head access to the magnetic surface. When the floppy disk is inserted into the floppy disk drive, the envelope remains stationary while the disk turns inside of it. Do *not* touch the mylar film. Touching the film or exposing it to grease or dirt can cause damage to any data stored on the disk.

In UNIX systems, floppy disks are used to introduce new software into the system or to archive selected items from the system's hard disks.

Tapes In many UNIX installations, particularly large systems that are operated by computer specialists, data is archived (backed up) on magnetic tape. Special tape recorders are used to store and replay data. If your system does not have a tape recorder, you ought to consider purchasing one. The hard disks used with the computer can hold a lot of data. You should periodically save the contents of the hard disk onto tape or floppy disks. Tape is more practical because floppy disks hold only a few hundred thousand bytes each.

Terminals

Your operating system manages the communications between your terminal and the computer. The terminal consists of a *keyboard* and a *video screen*. You communicate with the computer through your terminal. You "talk" to the computer via the keyboard, it "talks" to you via the video screen. Typical terminals display 24 lines of 80 characters each; some terminals can display as many as 132 characters on a single line.

The keyboard of a terminal is similar to the keyboard on a typewriter, but the computer keyboard has several keys the typewriter keyboard does not (see Figure 1-4). The number and location of these extra keys will vary from terminal to terminal.

Certain keys, however, will be found on most computer keyboards. These keys include the Escape, Control, Break, Delete, Backspace, and cursor control keys. Each of these keys gives a command to the computer. The control key is particularly useful. It is used in combination with the letter keys on your keyboard in a manner similar to that

of the shift key on the typewriter. When the control key is used with a letter key, such as a "d," the computer recognizes the combination as a unique command.

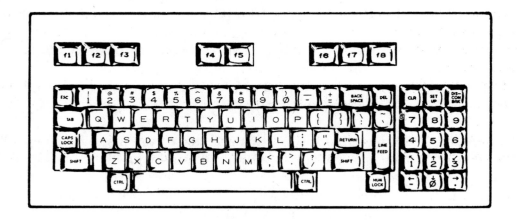

Figure 1-4 Keyboard

Printers

The operating system controls the communication between the printers and the computer. It also allocates the printing resources among the various users of the computer system. There are two basic kinds of printers used with computers: *character printers* and *line printers*. A character printer prints one character at a time (like a typewriter). A line printer prints an entire line at a time. Your computer many have more than one printer. If more than one printer is connected to the computer, they may be of different types.

Line printers are usually much faster (and much more expensive) than character printers. Print speeds of 300 and 600 lines per minute (LPM) are common. 600 lines per minute translates to approximately nine pages a minute. Line printers can either be connected to the computer directly or by a telephone connection.

Character printers now come in several forms: daisy wheel, dot matrix, ink jet, and laser. The daisy wheel printer usually provides the highest quality print. It is also the slowest (and the noisiest). It is essentially a typewriter modified for use with a computer.

The dot matrix printer forms letters through combinations of small dots. The print speed is much faster than that of a daisy wheel printer, but the variation in the print quality of dot matrix printers is considerable. Most new dot matrix printers offer a letter quality mode that would be acceptable for correspondence.

Ink jet printers offer a good combination of speed and quality. They are very quiet in operation and may be a good choice for an office environment—if for no other reason than noise.

Laser printers are high quality, fast, quiet, and expensive. They are normally used where print volumes are high and the print quality requirements rule out line printers.

Modems

Printers and terminals may be located some distance from the computer—as far away as the other side of the world. When they are, these peripherals have modems that connect them to the computer itself via the telephone system. Unless special lines are used, the rate at which information can be transferred will be much slower than when the peripherals are connected directly to the computer. Typical communications rates for modems are 30 and 120 characters per second (300 and 1200 baud).

THE OPERATING SYSTEM

UNIX is the glue that holds all of these pieces together. It is the control program for your computer. It schedules tasks, controls communications, and manages all of the computer's resources. It keeps track of what is stored on the disks, and where each item of information is located. In addition, it provides you with a set of tools that will allow you to get more from your computer.

In addition to controlling the computer, UNIX provides you with a whole set of utility programs that you (or your programmer) can use to format, display, sort, print, and search information. It provides a means for communicating with others who are using the computer. It provides a convenient way to leave notes or messages for co-

workers. And it provides you with a way to share large pools of information—such as inventory databases—with others who can profit from having access to such data.

UNIX has been called the "Once and Future Operating System." It has been a favorite of the avant garde computer science community for well over a decade, and it now seems destined to be the standard operating system of the future. There is little real competition for UNIX; most of the contending operating systems are little more than variations on the UNIX theme.

Because UNIX has been around a long time, there are many experienced computer users who are familiar with UNIX. Many books have been written about it—with good reason. UNIX was created as a professional user's operating system—the friendly users. It wasn't designed for the office environment. Even so, it can—and will—be used in the office.

Although UNIX has a reputation for being difficult to learn and use, this reputation is unfounded. As we'll see in this book, there is no reason to consider UNIX anything other than a simple set of rules for using and operating a computer. If there is any justifiable criticism of the UNIX system, it's that it sometimes appears to be just a little quaint and old-fashioned.

UNIX was created at AT&T's Bell Laboratories in 1969. The guiding light for its development was a fellow by the name of Ken Thompson. Thompson was soon joined by Dennis Ritchie (the creator of the C programming language). Together, they rewrote the original version of UNIX in C; this gave UNIX the potential to be a *portable* operating system—a system that could be used on a number of different kinds of computer systems. It is portability that is making UNIX into the operating system of tomorrow.

When hardware manufacturers build a computer, it needs an operating system. It can be much cheaper for the manufacturers to buy the basic system and tailor it to their hardware than to design an operating system from scratch. In addition, if the manufacturer chooses a widely used operating system, a large library of software becomes immediately available to the purchaser. This, in turn, makes the computer more marketable.

When the 32-bit super microcomputers began to appear, it made sense for the makers of these machines to use UNIX for their operating system. It was there, it worked, and it had a large library of software. It was also multi-user and multi-tasking.

Other than for a few specialized applications, there is no reason to manufacture 32-bit computers that are not multi-user computers.

When UNIX was developed, most computers were still fed by punched cards and were operated in a batch mode, where the computer does one task at a time. Computers have come a long way since then. UNIX led the way. UNIX was among the first multi-user, multi-tasking, and interactive operating systems.

Growth came slowly by today's standards. By 1974, UNIX was being used on over 600 computer installations. That was a lot in 1974. A good share of these were in the computer science departments of colleges and universities, which meant that a number of computer science graduates obtained a basic part of their training on the UNIX operating system. As these graduates entered the world of business and industry, they advocated the use of UNIX. After all, what you're familiar with always seems better than the alternatives.

Businesses, however, were not quite so ready to adopt UNIX into their data processing departments. Most DP managers were unsure about AT&T's commitment to UNIX—as were many university computer science departments. In those days, AT&T was in the telephone business, not the computer business. At the University of California in Berkeley, a major variation of UNIX was developed and some important contributions to UNIX were made. The Berkeley UNIX became popular in some parts of the user community.

The AT&T decision to enter the computer manufacturing business resolved any doubt about the company's commitment to UNIX. This decision, together with the fact that most of the other manufacturers had nowhere else to go, has made UNIX the operating system we will use today and tomorrow.

CHAPTER TWO

LOGGING IN

The person in your office or company who is in charge of your UNIX computer is called the system administrator. (If you are that person, you should read Appendix 2 at this time.) The system administrator assigns you a *login name* and an initial *password*.

Your UNIX system is a multi-user system. Your login name and password prevent unauthorized people from using the computer and browsing through your private data. They identify you as an authorized user of the computer.

GETTING INTO UNIX

Turn on your terminal. Be sure that the terminal is connected to the computer and that the computer is turned on. Press the Return key to let the computer know you're there. Your terminal should now display the word "Console login: " as shown below or simply "login:". The cursor will be positioned just after the word "login:". The cursor, which is indicated here by □, is the computer's equivalent to a pencil point. You can write on the screen at the point the cursor is located.

CHAPTER TWO

```
Console login: □
```

There may be a message on the line above "login." This message will vary from system to system. The specific screen displays shown in this book are for UNIX System V as delivered with the AT&T 3B2 computer. Remember that there may be slight differences in the display, depending upon the manufacturer or vendor of the machine. Don't be alarmed if your UNIX computer displays are not identical to the ones shown in this book.

The computer is waiting for you to enter your login name. Information you will enter is shown in boldface type in the sample screens. My login name is "byers". Note that it is all lowercase. The computer will not accept BYERS or Byers. Because UNIX discriminates between uppercase and lowercase, these would be different login names. Press the Return key after you have entered your login name.

```
Console Login: byers
Password: □
```

UNIX is a command-driven system, and so you must indicate to the computer that you have done something. The commands and parameters that you will enter are of different lengths, so you tell the computer when you have finished with your entry by pressing the Return key. The Return key gets its name from the return key on a typewriter. It should probably be labeled "Enter" or "Accept," but most terminals still use "Return."

Figure 2-1 Return Key

After you have entered your login name and pressed Return, you will be prompted to enter your *password*. The characters will not appear on the screen when you enter your password. This feature prevents someone from learning your password by glancing at the screen. When you have finished entering your password, press the Return key. (Remember that your password must be in exactly the same case as the password stored in the computer.)

If you've entered the correct login name and password, the screen display will look something like the one shown below.

```
Console Login: byers
Password:
UNIX SYSTEM RELEASE 5.3
No mail
$ □
```

The dollar sign ($) is the UNIX system prompt. Don't be alarmed if your system prompt is different from the "$." The prompt can be made to be whatever you want it to be. The prompt is UNIX's way of saying, "I'm ready, tell me what to do." The message above the prompt is the UNIX system message, and it is determined by the system administrator. It may change from time to time, depending on how energetic your system administrator is.

If you've made an error, the computer will display the message "Login incorrect" and prompt you to repeat the login procedure, shown below. Don't be concerned if you log in incorrectly; UNIX will let you keep trying until you get it right. Computers are very patient. Some computer systems, however, are configured to limit the number of trials you are allowed.

```
Console Login: byers
Password:
Login incorrect
Console Login: □
```

GETTING OUT OF UNIX

To get out of UNIX you will need to use the Control key. This key is usually found at the far left edge of the main part of the keyboard. It is sometimes labeled "CTRL." The caret (^) is often used to indicate the Control key in text. This key is used in the same way that you use the shift key. Holding down the shift key while you press the D key produces a capital "D." Holding down the Control key while you press the D key gets you out of UNIX. (The command Control -D will be indicated in the displays of this book by ^**D**.)

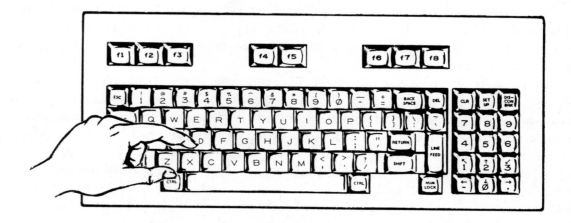

Figure 2-6 Control and D keys

Press Control and D (^D) together. The computer responds by prompting you to log in.

```
Console Login: byers
Password:
UNIX SYSTEM RELEASE 5.3
Console Login: □
```

Generally, it is important to log out of UNIX. Many UNIX installations charge users for time spent on the system. If this is the case, you are charged for the time from login to logout. Turning off your terminal or disconnecting your modem is not the same as logging out. In some installations, disconnecting the modem will log you off the system automatically. In others, the next user calling in will be automatically logged in as you—and you will be charged for that person's computer time. In the case where your terminal is always connected and you don't have time charges, anyone can turn on your terminal and use your data if you haven't logged out.

CHAPTER TWO

Now that you can get in and out of UNIX, you are ready to have it do something for you. A good first step is to change the password assigned to you by the system administrator. Start by logging back into UNIX using your initial password. Next, type the word **passwd** (all lowercase) after the prompt, and press Return. You are telling UNIX to execute the program named **passwd** (password).

Next, concerned as ever about security, UNIX will ask you to enter your existing password. This step is intended to prevent someone else from changing your password.

When you have successfully typed in your existing password, you are prompted to enter the new password. A password can be up to eight characters long. You cannot use the characters "@" or "#" in a password. You can use any other printable characters. Your password *must* be at least four characters long. If it is all lowercase or uppercase letters, it must be at least six characters long. If your password isn't acceptable to UNIX, you will be prompted to choose another. If security is important, it is recommended that your password be at least six characters long and that you use a mix of uppercase letters, lowercase letters, and numbers.

After you have entered your new password, you will be prompted to re-enter it. Because you cannot see the password as you enter it (more security measures), retyping it will reveal any typos in the original. If you enter exactly the same password twice, the system will accept your new password and this will be the password to use when you next log on. The transaction for changing your password is shown below.

```
$ passwd
Changing password for byers
old password:
new password:
retype new password:
$ □
```

UTILITY PROGRAMS

UNIX has large library of utility programs, and this library is available to you whenever you are using UNIX. **passwd** is an example of a UNIX utility program.

You use a utility program by simply typing the program name after a UNIX prompt. The names of the utility programs are the UNIX *commands*.

One of the advantages of a UNIX-operated computer is that you can send messages to other users of the computer. There are two ways to do this: You can use the **mail** utility to leave someone a note or you can send a message directly to their terminal with the **write** utility. To use either of these programs you *must* know the login name of the other party. A way to get login names—other than by simply asking someone—is to use **who**.

Who Else Is Using the Computer

who provides a list of everyone who is currently using the computer. A typical **who** listing is shown below.

```
$ who
alice          tty4     Aug 6    08:00:09
bob            tty1     Aug 3    12:22:15
byers          tty5     Aug 6    13:45:17
carol          tty2     Aug 6    08:11:36
ted            tty3     Aug 6    08:15:21
```

The first column contains the login names of the people using the system. The second column gives UNIX's name for their terminals (*ttyname*). Last is the date and time that they signed on to the system. Note that "bob" has been signed on for three days. He probably didn't log off as he should have on Friday night.

Sending and Receiving Mail

You can send a note to any user of the system at any time. They do not have to be using the computer when you send your message if you use the **mail** command. You must, however, know the recipient's login name. While you are getting started, it's probably best to send mail to yourself. It works just like sending it to anyone else. Of course, you could always send mail to some stranger from the **who** list.

To send mail to yourself, type the command **mail** followed by a space and then your login name. Then press Return. The cursor is positioned at the beginning of the next line. Just type in your message. When you have finished, press **^D** (Control -D) to tell UNIX that you have finished writing your message. This use of **^D** returns you to the UNIX prompt.

```
$ mail byers
This is a test of sending mail
to myself via the mail command.
Hope to hear from me soon.  RAB
$ □
```

To read your mail, type **mail** and press Return after a prompt. UNIX will display any waiting messages one at a time, as shown below. I sent this message to myself. Note that **mail** tells you who sent the message and when it was sent. At the end of the message, the cursor is positioned just to the right of a question mark.

To see the next message, if any, press Return.

```
$ mail
From byers   Mon Aug 6 15:30 PST 1984
To:   byers

This is a test of sending mail
to myself via the mail command.
Hope to hear from me soon.  RAB
? □
```

The question mark is the mail system's prompt. Type another "?" and press Return to get a list of the things that UNIX will let you do with your mail.

```
q                quit
x                exit without changing mail
p                print
s [file]         save (default mbox)
w [file]         same without header
—                print previous
d                delete
+                next (no delete)
m [user]         mail to user
! cmd            execute cmd
```

Sending and Receiving Messages

With UNIX, you can easily communicate with your co-workers, even if they are some distance away—such as in the south of France. Of course, if they are in the next room, it's easier to visit them in person.

You can carry on a conversation with another user of the system using the command **write**. To send a message, type the command **write**, a space, and the login name of the person for whom the message is intended. The cursor will be positioned on the line immediately below the **write** command. Type your message. The UNIX manual recommends that you use the letter "o" at the end of each part of your message to signal to the other party that you have finished and are waiting for an answer.

```
$ write carol
Have we shipped the Burns order yet? o
```

You should now wait for carol's response before sending another part of the message. Unix will display the message

```
Message from byers Mon Aug 6 15:45:23
Have we shipped the Burns order yet? o
```

on carol's terminal. If carol does respond, she must also use the **write** command. Once she has entered **write**, the dialogue can continue one line at a time until the

communication has been completed. When finished with **write**, press **^D**. This will return you to the UNIX prompt and display EOT (end of transmission) on the other party's terminal. The other party must also use **^D** to exit from **write**.

Life Without Messages

There are always times when we want to work without interruption. We can keep our friends and colleagues from bothering us by "taking the phone off the hook." Typing the command

```
$ mesg n
```

will accomplish this on the UNIX system. Anyone attempting to **write** to you will be informed that they cannot communicate with you at this time. The command

```
$ mesg y
```

will restore communications.

In this chapter you have learned to *log in* to UNIX and how to *log out* of UNIX. You've learned about passwords and how to change yours. You've learned that there are UNIX programs that you can use like commands. The **who** program provides a way to find out who else might be using the computer. With the **write** command, you can send messages back and forth to others who are on the system. You can use the **mail** command to leave notes for colleagues to read at a later time. You can become incommunicado by means of the **mesg** command. These are the basic communications tools for you and your colleagues on your UNIX-operated computer.

CHAPTER THREE

DISK DIRECTORIES

B oth the programs that help you work with the computer and the data and text files that result from your work with the computer are stored in *disk files*. A UNIX disk file can be as large as one billion bytes, which is equivalent to more than 300,000 standard 8 1/2 by 11 pages with one-inch margins. Each file on your disk has a *filename*. The filename was attached to the file when it was created. Each filename can be up to 14 characters long and can contain letters, numbers, underscores, periods, and commas. Some examples of valid UNIX filenames are:

Memorandum	LettertoEd
MEMORANDUM	Bank_Statement
memorandum	accounts.dbf
	invoice.A67213

Unlike many operating systems, UNIX discriminates between uppercase and lowercase letters. The three variations of "memorandum" shown above are three separate files under UNIX.

Many applications programs reserve a part of the filename for their own use. Most often, the applications program ends the filename with a period and one or more

characters. This is called a *file extension*. The dBASE II®applications program uses a period and three characters as its file extension. The file extension allows the applications program to identify files that are to be processed or handled in some unique way. The file extension does not, however, increase the total size of the filename. If your applications program uses file extensions, the number of characters allowed in your part of the filename will be reduced by the amount the application programs uses.

DIRECTORIES

UNIX keeps a list of the names of all of the files that are on the disk. This list is called the *disk directory*. The disk directory is itself a kind of disk file, which you use to display the names of the files that are on the disk.

UNIX computers are intended to be used by a number of people at the same time. The disk files for all of the users are cataloged in the UNIX disk directory. There can be thousands of files on the disk. Some of these files are *public* and can be used by everyone on the system; other files are *private* and are the property of an individual user; and still others are used only by UNIX itself.

The disk directory is organized into a number of smaller *subdirectories* in order to make it helpful to system users. Each of the subdirectories serves a particular user or task. Each subdirectory has a filename. These subdirectories are arranged into the hierarchy shown by Figure 3-1. The top box in our disk hierarchy is called the *root* (indicated by the symbol /), because the hierarchical diagram resembles an upside-down tree. Such hierarchical structures are often called tree structures.

DISK DIRECTORIES

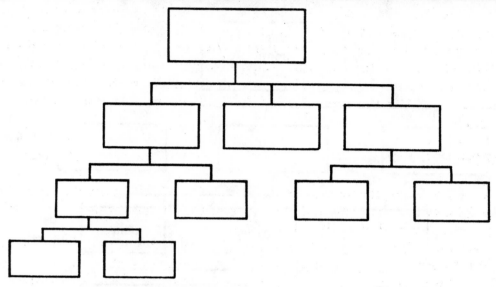

Figure 3-1 Diagram of a typical home directory

Another analogy for the organization of the disk directory is the management structure of a large corporation. The company president manages the firm through a number of vice-presidents. In turn, each vice-president works through a number of managers. Each manager works with supervisors and each supervisor is responsible for a group of workers. No single manager supervises a large number of workers directly.

When you log into UNIX you are automatically placed in your own directory. This directory is called your *home directory* and contains only the names of your private files. No one else can use these files unless you give them permission. (Automatic access permissions depend on your system's setup.) Your home directory is a subdirectory of the disk directory and its name is generally your *login name*. Your home directory, and all of the other users' home directories, usually belong to the "usr" system directory. Its place in the directory hierarchy is shown in Figure 3-2.

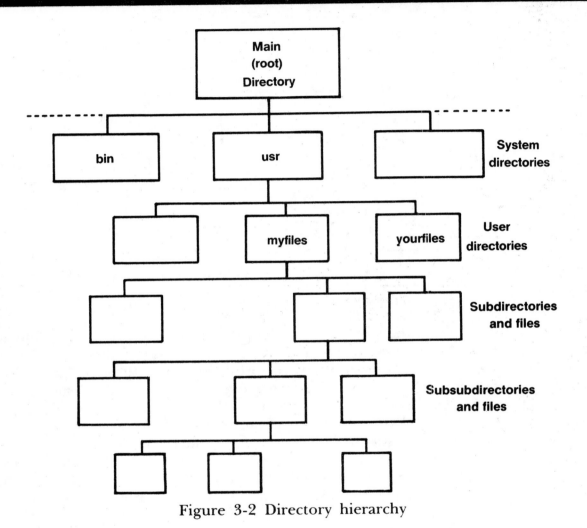

Figure 3-2 Directory hierarchy

Viewing the Contents of a Directory

To display the filenames stored in your directory, use the command **ls** (list). A typical display of filenames is shown below.

```
$ ls
arma.lite
contents
letter1
letter2
unix.ch3
```

The filenames are displayed in alphabetical order in a single column.

The filenames displayed may be ordinary files or they may be the names of your own subdirectories. The **ls** command does not discriminate between the two. Use

```
$ ls -l
```

to determine which files are directories. This command will display the names of all of the files in a single column with other information about the file displayed to the left of the filename. If the first character on the line of the filename is a "d," the file is a directory. A "-" as the first character indicates that the file is an ordinary one.

Filenames beginning with a period (.) are not normally displayed. The command

```
$ ls -a
```

allows you to view these *invisible* filenames. The **a** and **l** options can be combined as in **ls -al**. If there are many filenames in your directory, the **ls** command can restrict the display to names which match certain criteria. For example,

```
$ ls m*
```

displays only those filenames that begin with the letter "m." The star (*) is a *wildcard*. This instructs UNIX to use any sequence of characters. The question mark (?) is another wildcard. Use

```
$ ls ???L*
```

and the display shows the names of all files where the fourth character is an "L." Using

```
$ ls *L*
```

results in the display of all filenames that contain the letter "L."

Square brackets ([]) are used to indicate classes of characters. The command

```
$ ls [abc]*
```

will display all filenames beginning with either "a," "b," or "c." Perhaps you assign identification numbers to files. For example, you might identify business letters as "letter1," "letter2," and so on. The dash (-) can be used to specify a range of characters (letters or numbers). The command

```
$ ls letter[1-5]
```

will display all filenames beginning with "letter" and ending with the numbers 1 through 5. Similarly, use

```
$ ls [a-c]*
```

to display filenames beginning with the letters a through c.

Paths and Pathnames

You can display filenames contained in other directories— provided that you are authorized to use those directories. This brings us to *paths* and *pathnames*. In Figure 3-3, a path traces a route from the *root directory* to a particular file. The path to the file "AT1" is outlined by heavy black lines. The pathname consists of the names of all of the directories, in from the root to—and including—the particular file. The names are separated by slashes. For example,

```
/usr/myfiles/correspondence/AT1
```

is the complete, or *absolute pathname*, for the file "AT1." The command

$$\$ \ \textsf{ls} \ \ /\textsf{usr}/\textsf{myfiles}/\textsf{correspondence}$$

will display the names of all of the files that are in the directory "correspondence." This may seem somewhat elaborate and awkward, but it does get the job done. You can always use the absolute pathname in a command.

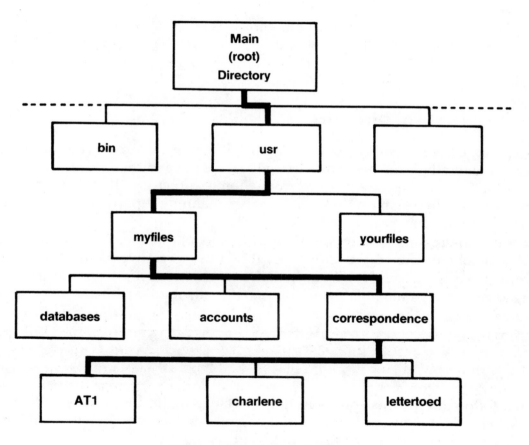

Figure 3-3 Path diagram

Whenever the directory that you are using—that is, your working directory—is on the same path and above another file or directory, you can use a *relative pathname* for those files. The relative pathname consists of the names of the files below the directory you are working in. For example, if you are working in the directory "myfiles,"

        correspondence/AT1

is the relative pathname for the file "AT1." If you wish to view names of all of the files in the directory "correspondence," use

        $ ls correspondence

to display them.

Making Your Own Directory

You can create a subdirectory anywhere in the hierarchy below your home directory. Generally, you are not allowed to create a directory above your home directory or on another path from your home directory. Keeping each of your directories to smaller than one screenful makes scanning a particular directory easier, and the computer can search it more quickly.

In order to create a directory, you must use its pathname. You can use either the *absolute* pathname or the *relative* pathname. If you use a relative pathname, be sure that you are in the right directory. To ask UNIX, "Where am I?", use the **pwd** (present working directory) command. **pwd** displays the absolute pathname of your current directory.

```
$ pwd
/usr/myfiles
```

Let's follow the process of creating a directory by making a new subdirectory of "myfiles" with the **mkdir** (make directory) command. The new directory will be named "unixbook." Use either the **mkdir** command

$ mkdir /usr/myfiles/unixbook

(with the absolute pathname) or

$ mkdir unixbook

(with the relative pathname).

Deleting a Directory

Before you can delete (erase) a directory, it must be empty. It cannot contain the names of any files or subdirectories. Further, you cannot erase the directory currently in use, and you cannot delete your home directory. The command used is **rmdir** (remove directory) and

$ rmdir *pathname_of_directory*

is its syntax. Either the absolute pathname or the relative pathname can be used when deleting directories. For example, to delete the empty directory "oldstuff" from "myfiles" use either

$ rmdir /usr/myfiles/oldstuff

or

$ rmdir oldstuff

if you are currently in "myfiles."

Selecting a Different Working Directory

You can designate any of your subdirectories as your working directory. This option can save both aggravation and typing because it allows you to refer to files in your current directory by their ordinary filenames. You must refer to files in subdirectories by their pathnames. The command to select another directory as your working directory is **cd** (change directory). with

> **cd** *name_of_new_working_directory*

as the syntax. For example, you can use

> $ **cd unixbook**

to select "unixbook" as your working directory. You can use either

> $ **cd /usr/myfiles**

or

> $ **cd ..**

to return to using "myfiles" as your working directory. The ".." is a built-in UNIX shorthand for the next higher directory. You cannot move to a directory that you are not authorized to use.

This chapter has shown you how disk directories allow you to find files on the disk. The command **ls** gives a listing of all of the files in a directory. The **pwd** command shows the pathname of the current directory. **cd** allows you to change from one directory to another. The command **mkdir** creates a new directory. Delete an empty directory with **rmdir**.

CHAPTER FOUR

WORKING WITH UNIX DISK FILES

The UNIX operating system provides a means to display the names of the files on the disk, to make copies of files, to erase files, to rename files, and to view the contents of files on the terminal or printer. There are many reasons for making a copy of a file. You may want to keep a copy of an original draft of a document prior to editing. You may want to move files from a directory to a subdirectory.

COPYING FILES

UNIX has two commands that can be used to copy files: **mv** (move) and **cp** (copy). Entering the command line

```
$ cp unix.ch3 unix.ch3.bak
```

will make a copy of the file "unix.ch3" named "unix.ch3.bak." The disk now contains the two files "unix.ch3" and "unix.ch3.bak." The copy command requires that you first name the file to be copied (the source file) and then the name of the new file (the target file). The form, or syntax, of the **cp** command is:

```
cp  filename_to_be_copied  filename_of_copy
```

The command

```
$ cp unix* unixbook
```

will copy all of the files beginning with "unix" to the new directory "unixbook." Both the home directory "myfiles" and the subdirectory "unixbook" now contain copies of all files beginning with "unix." The form of this command is:

```
cp  filename(s)_to_be_copied name_of_target_directory
```

You can also use the **mv** command to move a file from one directory to another. In the example,

```
$ mv unix* unixbook
```

we move all of the files with names beginning with "unix" from "myfiles" to "unixbook." "myfiles" does *not* contain a duplicate copy of those files. The syntax of the **mv** command is:

```
mv  filename(s)_to_be_moved name_of_target_directory
```

CHANGING A FILENAME

From time to time, you may wish to change the name of a file. Surprisingly, the **mv** command accomplishes the change. The command below will change the name of the file "gloss" to "glossary."

```
$ mv gloss glossary
```

The syntax of the **mv** command is

```
mv name_to_be_changed  new_name
```

when you use it to rename a file.

ERASING A FILE

Y ou can also remove a filename from the disk directory. When you do this, the file itself is removed from the disk, and the space that it occupied is made available for other files. You should clean up your directories regularly and remove disk files that you no longer need. Disk space is a valuable commodity, particularly in systems with a single hard disk drive.

Removing an ordinary disk file is accomplished with the **rm** (remove) command. Use **rm** in this way:

```
rm filename(s)_to_be_removed
```

The command

```
$ rm unix.bak
```

will erase the file "unix.bak" from the current (working) directory. To erase the file "unix.bak" from the subdirectory "unixbook," use

```
$ rm unixbook/unix.bak
```

FINDING A FILE

S ooner or later, you will have a large assortment of files spread over several directories. How do you find a file when you have forgotten which directory it's in? There are two ways: You can search each of your directories manually, or you can have UNIX **find** it for you. Manual searches are, simply, drudgery—and computers are supposed to help eliminate drudgery. The syntax

```
find pathname -name desired_filename -print
```

will instruct UNIX to search for the file. This command searches downward from the indicated directory for the desired file. If the file is found, its pathname will be displayed, provided that the **-print** option is included in the command.

Let's illustrate finding a file by looking for the file "unix.ch1," which is located in the directory "unixbook." This directory is a subset of the directory "myfiles," the working directory, so use the **pwd** command to obtain the pathname of the current directory. Then, use the **find** command to search downward beginning with that directory:

```
$ pwd
/usr/myfiles
$ find /usr/myfiles -name unix.ch1 -print
/usr/myfiles/unixbook/unix.ch1
```

Or, you can save keystroke with:

```
$ find . -name unix.ch1 -print
```

The dot(.) is shorthand for the present working directory.

You can use the wildcard characters * and ? to locate a class of filenames. If you use wildcards, however, you must place the filename containing the wildcard in quotes. For example,

```
$ find /usr/myfiles -name "u*" -print
```

will display a list containing the location of all the filenames beginning with "u."

VIEWING A FILE ON YOUR TERMINAL

You can view the contents of your files directly on your terminal—without having to use an applications program. Displaying a file on your terminal is accomplished by the **cat** (catenate) and **pr** (print) commands. The syntax of **cat** is

```
cat filename
```

and so,

> `$ cat unix.ch1`

will allow you view the contents of the file "unix.ch1" on your terminal. The **cat** command can also be used to view several files in sequence; the command syntax is:

> `$ cat` *`list_of_filenames`*

The filenames must be separated from each other by spaces. For example, the command is

> `$ cat unix.ch1  unix.ch2  unix.ch3`

to view the files "unix.ch1," "unix.ch2," and "unix.ch3." If the display requires more than a single screenful, you can freeze the display by holding down the Control key while you press the S key (^**S**). To unfreeze the display, press ^**Q**.

You can also use **cat** to copy the contents of one or more files into another file. When you do this, the command takes the form

> `cat` *`file_list`* `>` *`target_filename`*

The command

> `$ cat unix.ch1 > example`

will copy the content of the file "unix.ch1" to the new file "example."

> `$ cat unix.ch1 unix.ch2 unix.ch3 > section1`

will combine the files "unix.ch1," "unix.ch2," and "unix.ch3" into a new file named "section1." It is important to note that you still have the files named "unix" on your disk in addition to the new files.

The **cat** command can also create a file into which data from the keyboard can be entered. This option gives you an easy way to leave notes for yourself. Omit the source filenames to create a file. For example, use the sequence

```
$ cat > ABC
This is the note that I'm leaving for myself
^D
```

to leave a note in the file "ABC." When you use **cat** in this way, you must press ^D to stop entering text.

ANOTHER WAY TO VIEW FILES

The **pr** (print) command displays a file on your terminal. The name of the command dates back to the days when computer users had printing terminals, not video terminals. Often, the **pr** command provides a more useful way to display files than **cat**. **pr** automatically separates the file into pages. Each page has a page header which consists of the date, the filename, and the page number.

> pr *option_list file_list*

is the form for the **pr** command.

The file list is simply a list of filenames separated by spaces. The option list allows you to specify exactly how you want the display formatted. You do not, however, need to list any options. The available formatting options include:

-n	Number of columns (this book is 1 column)
+n	Starting page number
-wn	n is the page width in spaces (default is 72)
-ln	n is the page length in lines (default is 66)
-t	Don't print the standard header
-m	Print the files simultaneously (one to a column)

Most modern terminals use 24 lines of 80 characters. For terminal display it is usually desirable to use an options list such as **-w80-l24-t**. This list will give you the most efficient use of your screen. The standard header, default page length, and width are really only valuable when using a printing terminal. Use

```
$ pr -w80 -l24 -t unix.ch1
```

to display the contents of the file "unix.ch1."

PRINTING A FILE

Use the **lp** command (line print) to print the contents of a file. On earlier versions of UNIX, the printing command was "lpr," the line printer command. When UNIX was designed, most computers used a single high-speed line printer. User terminals were printing terminals, not video terminals. A single, high-speed line printer was shared by all of the users and was used for high volume data output or for listings of large programs.

Today, the printing needs of computer users are more varied, ranging from correspondence printing on company letterhead to dumps of the current contents of large databases. The computer printer must handle this wide range of printing needs.

The **lp** command allows you to specify the kind of printer that you want to use. This option is only valuable if there is more than one kind of printer on your system. You can also specify the number of copies that you want printed.

With the command,

```
$ lp letter
```

printing the contents of the file "letter" is simple. This particular command will print the file using the *default* printer, which is the printer that is used if no printer is specified. If the default printer is already busy, the file will be held until the printer is available, which is called *spooling*. Spooling places all printing requests into a queue. Each file in the queue will be printed as the printer becomes available. When your file is placed in the queue, an identification code is sent back to your terminal. This identification code allows you to cancel the print request with the **cancel** command:

```
$ cancel id_code
```

You can also use the **lp** command to connect the printer to your keyboard, allowing you to print hardcopy without going through the process of creating a file. This is accomplished by using **lp** without specifying a filename. The cursor on your terminal will be positioned below the prompt, and you type your text just as you would on a typewriter. Press Control and D together to signal that you are finished. (Pressing ^D has many uses. Earlier we saw that it is used to logout of UNIX; here it signals that you have finished typing. Pressing ^D allows you to exit from the level of UNIX in which you are working.) The general syntax of the **lp** command is

```
lp option_list file_list
```

and the available options are:

-c   Makes a link to each file or makes a copy of each file in the file list. This allows the file to be printed even in the event that the files are deleted before they can be printed. If the option is *not* used, don't delete the files before they are printed.

-d   Allows you to specify a particular printer or a class of printer. For example, you may specify that you want the file to be printed by a letter quality printer located on the third floor. Each printer has a printer name and is assigned to a class of devices. The option has no value when there is only one printer attached to your computer. If there is more than one printer connected to your computer, contact your system administrator for a list of printer names and classes. You can also obtain information about your printers and their status with the **lpstat** (line print status) command with its **-t** option:

```
lpstat −t
```

-m	Sends a message via mail when the print request has been completed. This option is valuable when the printer is located some distance away from you and the print load is heavy enough so that printing may occur some time after the request.
-w	Same as **-m** except that the message is sent to the re-quester's terminal. If the requester is no longer logged in, mail is sent instead.
-n#	Allows you to specify when multiple copies are to be printed. Enter **-n** followed by the number of copies. A single copy is printed if this option is not used.
-o	Allows you to specify printer dependent or printer class dependent options when they exist. See your system administrator to learn which options exist on your computer (if any).
-t	A banner page (a leading page giving information about the file, the filename, and the requestor) is printed on many UNIX installations. This option allows you to specify a title for the banner page. Enter the title immediately after the **-t**. If more than one word is to be used in the title, enclose the title in quotes.

You can also use the **lp** command to print the results of other commands. For example, to print a directory, use the **ls** command with the **lp** command as shown below

```
$ ls | lp
```

The vertical bar (|) is known as a *pipe*. It is used to connect the output of the **ls** command as the input for the **lp** command. You could also use the **pr** command to do rough formatting for the **lp** command.

```
$ ls | pr -4 | lp
```

The above command string will take the output of the **ls** command, format it for four-column printing, and then print the output using the **lp** command.

In UNIX, data, text, and programs are stored on the disk as disk files. Each disk file has a *filename*. The filenames are recorded in a *disk directory*. The directory, which is itself a disk file, is arranged in a hierarchy of smaller *subdirectories*. The route from the topmost, or root, directory to a subdirectory is called a *path*. The complete name of an ordinary file or directory is its *pathname*. The pathname consists of all of the directory names, in order, from the root to the file. The filenames are separated by slashes.

In this chapter, you have seen that UNIX provides a number of commands to help you use and manipulate the disk files. With **rm**, you can remove a file from the disk. Files are copied with the **cp** command. You can use **mv** to move files from on directory to another; **mv** can also used to rename files. **find** allows you to locate the directories containing a particular filename. You can view the contents of a file on your terminal with either **cat** or **pr**. Also, **cat** can be used to group (catenate) several files into a single larger file. **pr** can format as well as display data. **lp** is used to display data on a printer. **lp** and **pr** can be used together to produce formatted data on your printer with a technique called *piping*.

CHAPTER FIVE

DATE AND TIME

Most modern computers contain a simple clock that continues to keep time even when the computer is turned off. Others require that someone enter the time and date when the system is turned on. UNIX offers a range of valuable commands to deal with time and dates. Most often, the *system clock* is used to keep track of when files are created or changed. Each time a change is made, the file is tagged with the current time and date. Displays and printouts made with the help of the **pr** (print) command have a page header that contains the current date and time.

DATE

The UNIX **date** command gives you the current system time and date:

```
$ date
Wed Aug 16 14:44:12  PDT  1984
```

Note that UNIX uses a 24-hour clock. Usually, only the system administrator can change the date and time with the **date** command. The system administrator can,

however, change the rwx (read, write, and execution) permissions of the command so that someone else can change the date and time. Use the command syntax

date *yymmddhhmm.ss*

to change the system date and time; year, month, day, hour, minute, and second are entered. The **yy** is the last two digits of the year, **mm** is the number for the current month. Each *must* be a two-digit entry. For example, "January" is represented as "01." Use a leading zero for any entry that would usually be represented as a one-digit number. The seconds entry is optional. If seconds are entered, the value must be preceded by a period. The command

$ date 8408270330

will set the clock to 3:30 P.M. August 27, 1984. The year, month, and day can be omitted. When they are, the current values are used. Thus, you can change the time without having to enter the date.

Calendars

For those who have difficulty remembering what year it is, UNIX can display a calendar for any year from A.D. 1 to A.D. 9999. Use the **cal** (calendar) command with the syntax

cal *month year*

to obtain the calendar. The month entry is optional. It is specified by a number between 1 and 12. However, when using the **cal** command, do not enter a leading zero if the number is less than 10. If you do not specify a month, the entire year calendar will be displayed. The year must be specified completely. For example, to display a calendar for 1984, you must enter all four digits of the year. Entering "84" will produce a calendar for the year 84, not 1984. Figure 5-1 shows the command for displaying a calendar for August, 1984.

```
$ cal 8 1984
   S  M Tu  W Th  F  S
                1  2  3  4
   5  6  7  8  9 10 11
  12 13 14 15 16 17 18
  19 20 21 22 23 24 25
  26 27 28 29 30 31
$
```

Figure 5-1 **cal**

To print the calendar you must combine the **cal** (calendar) command with the **lp** (line printer) command. For example, the command

$ cal 1776 | lp

will print the calendar for the year 1776 on the system printer. Remember, the vertical bar in the command is called a pipe. It is used to combine the two separate commands into a single command. In general, you will need to pipe a command with the **lp** command whenever you want printed output. (The 1776 Revolutionary War calendar printed by UNIX is shown in Figure 5-2.)

1776

		Jan								Feb								Mar				
S	M	Tu	W	Th	F	S	S	M	Tu	W	Th	F	S	S	M	Tu	W	Th	F	S
	1	2	3	4	5	6					1	2	3						1	2
7	8	9	10	11	12	13	4	5	6	7	8	9	10	3	4	5	6	7	8	9
14	15	16	17	18	19	20	11	12	13	14	15	16	17	10	11	12	13	14	15	16
21	22	23	24	25	26	27	18	19	20	21	22	23	24	17	18	19	20	21	22	23
28	29	30	31				25	26	27	28	29			24	25	26	27	28	29	30
														31						

		Apr								May								Jun				
S	M	Tu	W	Th	F	S	S	M	Tu	W	Th	F	S	S	M	Tu	W	Th	F	S
	1	2	3	4	5	6				1	2	3	4							1
7	8	9	10	11	12	13	5	6	7	8	9	10	11	2	3	4	5	6	7	8
14	15	16	17	18	19	20	12	13	14	15	16	17	18	9	10	11	12	13	14	15
21	22	23	24	25	26	27	19	20	21	22	23	24	25	16	17	18	19	20	21	22
28	29	30					26	27	28	29	30	31		23	24	25	26	27	28	29
														30						

		Jul								Aug								Sep				
S	M	Tu	W	Th	F	S	S	M	Tu	W	Th	F	S	S	M	Tu	W	Th	F	S
	1	2	3	4	5	6					1	2	3	1	2	3	4	5	6	7
7	8	9	10	11	12	13	4	5	6	7	8	9	10	8	9	10	11	12	13	14
14	15	16	17	18	19	20	11	12	13	14	15	16	17	15	16	17	18	19	20	21
21	22	23	24	25	26	27	18	19	20	21	22	23	24	22	23	24	25	26	27	28
28	29	30	31				25	26	27	28	29	30	31	29	30					

		Oct								Nov								Dec				
S	M	Tu	W	Th	F	S	S	M	Tu	W	Th	F	S	S	M	Tu	W	Th	F	S
		1	2	3	4	5						1	2	1	2	3	4	5	6	7
6	7	8	9	10	11	12	3	4	5	6	7	8	9	8	9	10	11	12	13	14
13	14	15	16	17	18	19	10	11	12	13	14	15	16	15	16	17	18	19	20	21
20	21	22	23	24	25	26	17	18	19	20	21	22	23	22	23	24	25	26	27	28
27	28	29	30	31			24	25	26	27	28	29	30	29	30	31				

Figure 5-2 1776 Revolutionary War Calendar

Reminders

UNIX also provides a reminder service with the **calendar** command. To use this calendar service, you must have a file named "calendar." This file should be located on your home (login) directory. To illustrate the use of this command, let's create the file "calendar" and store a reminder message in the file. We can create this file using the **cat** (catenate) command. You can also use a commercial word processor or any of the UNIX text processors, such as the **ed** or **vi** editors (see Chapter 7 and Appendix 1), to create the file "calendar." Our sample message is stored into the file "calendar":

```
$ cat > calendar
Charlene's birthday is Sept 4
^D
$
```

The result of the **calendar** command will now depend on the day the command is used. **calendar** scans the file "calendar" and displays any messages containing either today's or tomorrow's date. Monday is considered to be tomorrow on Friday. In this example, the message will be displayed on both September 3rd and 4th. Because the 4th occurs on a Monday in 1984, the message will also be displayed on Friday, September 1st.

If the message contains more than one line, the date must appear on each line of the message. The month must precede the day. A date, such as "September 4" can appear in any of several forms:

9/4
Sept 4
september 4

Many UNIX systems use the **calendar** command to provide an automatic reminder service for all users. For this to function, your calendar file must be public, and it must be located on your home directory. Then the system will use **calendar** to read your calendar file at night and send you any messages via the mail system. When you log into UNIX, you are informed whether or not you have mail.

TIME

You can have UNIX execute a command or a series of commands at any specified time. Such a feature has many uses. For example, you can use this feature to send yourself a reminder message at a specific time. Suppose you have a meeting at 3:15 and you will be working with the computer until then. You could create the message (using **cat**) and have your computer remind you at 3 o'clock.

```
$ cat > bob
You have a 3:15 Meeting with Wayne
^D
$
```

To send yourself a message at 3 o'clock in the afternoon, use the **at** command. The **at** command cannot direct the output to the screen. So, we use the **mail** command. The form of this command is

> **at** *time filename*

with the filename optional. The **at** command is used when you already have a file containing the commands that you want executed later. If the filename is omitted, you will be placed in a text entry mode. While in this mode, you can enter one or more commands, one to a line. To exit the mode, use **^D**. The command sequence is

```
$ at 3pm
mail byers < bob
^D
$
```

to display the reminder at 3 P.M. The time can use either the 24-hour clock or the 12-hour clock. UNIX interprets one-digit and two-digit numbers as hours; three-digit and four-digit numbers as hours and minutes. If the time is not followed by "am" or "pm," UNIX will assume the time is on the 24-hour scale. If "pm" were omitted from this example, the computer would send you the message at 3 in the morning.

DATE AND TIME

Another practical use for the **at** command is for scheduling an activity that requires particularly heavy use of the computer's resources for the middle of the night when there will be little interference from or with other users. This feature is advantageous on computers that employ time charges. These systems often have a much lower time charging rate at night—as an incentive to level the computer's work load.

The general syntax of the **at** command allows you to execute a command at an arbitrary date and time—up to a year later. The **at** syntax is

      at *time date filename*

with the date optional. The date can consist of a month and day (e.g., 7/28) or a day of the week (e.g., friday). You can use any of the standard abbreviations for the month. The day of the week can also be abbreviated.

Timing Commands

It's sometimes useful to know how long it takes to perform a particular operation, such as sorting. On a single-user personal computer, it is relatively easy to determine. You use a stop watch and measure how long it takes. This is called *wall clock* time. With a multi-user system like UNIX, wall clock time doesn't always give you the answer. The computer resources that are devoted to your job will depend on a number of factors, such as how many people are using your computer and what they are doing. The **time** command has the syntax

      time *command filename*

and it provides you with three versions of the time required to execute the command: the elapsed (wall clock) time, the time spent in the system, and the actual execution time. Perhaps we wish to determine the actual execution time taken to sort a large file. The filename of our large file is "inventory." The command

      $ time sort inventory

will time this operation.

50

This chapter has covered the UNIX commands that concern time and dates. **date** provides you with the current time and date. The **cal** command can be used to display or print a calendar for any year from A.D. 1 to A.D. 9999 (a long time). The command **calendar** provides you with an automatic reminder service. You can time a particular operation with the **time** command. The **at** command can set a timer to execute a command at a specific future time. The execution time can be months later.

CHAPTER SIX

SHARING FILES

One of the major virtues of UNIX is that it allows you to share information with the other users of your computer system—because a single copy of a file, such as an inventory database, can be used by everyone. Of course, you may not want to share all of your files. When you create a file, you are the *owner* of that file. UNIX allows you to choose which files you want to share and with whom they are to be shared. For each file you *own*, you can choose to:

- Keep the file as your private property.
- Share the file with only the members of a group.
- Share the file with everyone.

A *group* consists of a specific list of users. The group is usually established by your system administrator, who assigns a *group id* to all of the members of the group. The members of your group are usually project personnel or people from the same department. You might not belong to any group or you might belong to several groups.

When you use a file, three operations are possible: *read, write,* and *execute*. Reading means that you can look at or use the contents of a file. Writing to a file means that you

can add to or change the content of the file. Executing means you can run those files that are computer programs or search those files that are directories. Reading, writing, and executing are independent features. For example, you can allow others to read one of your files while prohibiting them from changing the file.

ACCESS PERMISSIONS

The privileges of reading, writing, and executing (or searching) are known as the *access permissions*. Access permissions are separately assigned for yourself, the members of your group, and everyone else. There are a total of nine possible access permissions. When you create a file, a *default* set of access permissions is automatically assigned for that file.

You can find out what the access permissions are for any of your files with the **ls** (list) command and the syntax

ls −l *filename(pathname)*

For example, you would use

$ ls −l unixbook/unix.ch1

to view the access permission to the file "unix.ch1" in your subdirectory "unixbook." Your UNIX computer will respond with

−rw−r−−r−− 1 myfiles 4096 Aug 16 14:23:16 unix.ch1

or something similar. The first block of characters, -rw-r--r--, is called the *mode*. The mode describes the access permissions for the file and tells you whether or not the file is a directory. "myfiles" is the name of the owner of the file. The number "1," located between the mode and the owner's name, gives the number of links. (Links are discussed later in this chapter.) The number "4096" is the size of this file in bytes. The date and time indicate when the file was last changed. And, of course, "unix.ch1" is the name of the file.

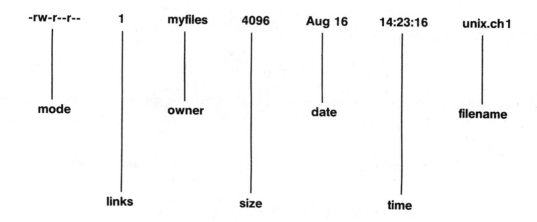

Figure 6-1 Diagram of parts of directory listing

Now let's look at the *mode*. The first character of the mode identifies the file type: A dash (-) indicates the file is an ordinary file. A "d" indicates that it is a directory. This file is an ordinary file because it begins with a dash (-). The next nine characters make up three three-character access permission blocks. These three blocks contain the access permissions for the file owner, members of the owner's group, and everyone else.

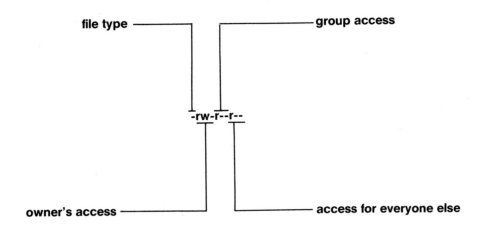

Figure 6-2 Diagram of mode

An "r" in the first position of a block indicates permission to *read* the file. A "w" in the second position of a block indicates permission to *write* to the file. An "x" in the third position of a block indicates permission to *execute* the file if it is a program or to *search* the file if it is a directory. The dash (-) indicates that permission is withheld. In this example, the owner may read and write to the file. Everyone else is only allowed to read the file.

Whenever you create a file, a set of access permissions is assigned to the file automatically. The specific permissions will vary from system to system (they can be changed by the system administrator). Many systems normally extend read permission to everyone and restrict write permission to the owner.

Changing Access Permissions

You are allowed to change the access permissions of the files that you own. These are the files that contain your *login name* in the owner's column when you do a directory

listing with the **ls -l** command. To change access permissions, use the command **chmod** (change mode). The command syntax

chmod *who=access filename*

will allow you to change access permissions on files you own. *who* is a code that describes which of the three access blocks is to be changed. The who code is constructed from the letters "u," "g," and "o":

u	user	(you, the file owner)
g	group	(your group)
o	other	(everyone else)

Access indicates the three-character access block. Let's change the access permissions so that our example file is the owner's private property. The command

$ chmod go-rwx unix.ch1

sets each of the three characters in the access blocks for your group and everyone else to "permission denied." Note that there is no blank space *before* or *after* the minus sign. The mode (as viewed with **ls -l**) looks like

```
-rw-------
```

Use the + (plus) or – (minus) sign to add or subtract access permissions in any combi—nation of r, w, or x.

You can also use the = (equal sign) to set the access permissions to any pattern. Let's change all three access permission blocks to read, write, and execute. The command

$ chmod ugo=rwx unix.ch1

changes the mode, and

```
-rwxrwxrwx
```

will be displayed.

By the way, you can protect your files from being accidentally erased by removing write privileges for all users—including yourself. Removing your own write privileges will not completely prevent you from changing the file, but the **rm** command *will* prompt you for confirmation. If you do remove these privileges, you must remember to reset the mode each time you want to make changes to the file.

SWITCHING GROUPS

You can belong to a number of different groups. When you log into the computer you are automatically placed into your primary group (if you belong to more than one group). If you do belong to more than one group, you can switch to one of your other group assignments in order to change group access permission for a particular file. The command is **newgrp** (newgroup). The syntax is

```
newgrp group_id
```

for switching to another group. Remember, all of your group id's are assigned by the system administrator.

TRANSFERRING FILE OWNERSHIP

It will occasionally be necessary to transfer the ownership of a file from one owner to another. The system administrator will accomplish this transfer with the UNIX command **chown** (change owner). The syntax of the command is

```
chown new_owner's_name filename
```

to change ownership of a file.

The new owner's name is usually the *login name* of one of the other users. For example, the command

```
$ chown sally unix.ch1
```

changes the ownership of the file "unix.ch1" to the person whose login name is "sally." You can also copy (**cp**) another user's file and you will be the owner of the copy.

CHANGING THE GROUP ID OF YOUR FILES

It may also be necessary, from time to time, to change the *group id* of your files. Just as with changing owners (**chown**), changing groups can only be accomplished by your system administrator. The UNIX command is **chgrp** (change group). The syntax of this command is

```
chgrp new_group_id filename
```

to change the group id for your files.

USING SOMEONE ELSE'S FILES

You can use a file that belongs to someone else, provided that you have been granted permission to do so. To use the other file, you will refer to it by its absolute pathname. This can be somewhat of a nuisance, particularly for files that you use often. For such files, you can create an entry in your own directory that is a *synonym* for the pathname of someone else's file. Using this synonym is the same as using the absolute pathname of the file you are sharing.

To illustrate, let's suppose that your friend sally has a file that you are permitted to use. For the sake of example, let's say that

```
/usr/sally/misc/popdata/census80/michigan
```

is the pathname for this file. It's not convenient to use this long pathname each time that you refer to the file. UNIX allows you to use a different name of your own choosing for *your* use of this file, provided that the file is *not* a directory. Use the **ln** (link) command to assign your own filename to a shared file. This command links your name to the file without changing the name assigned by the owner of the file. The syntax is

ln *pathname_to_link_to your_filename*

for the **ln** command. Use the command

ln /usr/sally/misc/popdata/census80/michigan mich.data

to make "mich.data" your synonym for the example pathname. There is still only *one* file. However, this file now has two names: the original name in the other directory and the synonym "mich.data," which is now a filename in your working directory. UNIX allows a file to have multiple filenames. These filenames exist apart from the file itself. The names are linked (tied) to the file by the **ln** command. Incidentally, your friend, sally, is still the owner of this file. The access permissions of the file remain unchanged, and you cannot alter them. The linkage is simply a matter of convenience for you. If you use **ls -l** for this file,

```
$ ls -l mich.data
-rw-r--r-- 2 sally  13406  Aug 16  14:23:16  mich.data
```

might be the display.

The "2" just before the owner's name represents the total number of links (synonyms) used for this file. If sally deletes this file, her filename will be removed from her directory. The file itself will still be on the disk. You will only know that she has deleted the file when you use **ls -l** and find that the number of links has changed to "1." sally remains the owner of the file even after she deletes it—and you still cannot change the access permissions. The file is deleted from the disk only when the last filename (synonym) linked to that file is deleted. Fortunately, because you have access permission to read the file, you can copy it. The copy will then be your own file and you can make changes to the access permissions.

In this chapter you have seen how to share information with other users of the UNIX computer, how to choose with whom to share information, and how to set the conditions for sharing. The commands **chmod** and **newgrp** determines who can use the information in our files and who can change it. **chown** reassigns the ownership of a file. **chgrp** reassigns the group affiliation of a file. **ln** allows the same file to have more than one name.

CHAPTER SEVEN

TEXT EDITING AND FORMATTING

UNIX has a built-in program, called **ed** (editor), with which you can enter and edit text. Some UNIX systems also have an additional editor, **vi** (visual editor). There are two basic kinds of text editors: line and screen. **ed** is a line editor. **vi** is a screen editor. With a line editor, you work with a single line at a time. With a screen editor, you work with as much text as will fit on your terminal screen at a time. Screen editors work best when the terminal is connected directly to the computer; line editors are most useful when you are connected to the computer via a modem. **ed** or **vi** can be used along with the formatting programs **nroff** and **troff** to perform the equivalent of word processing. This chapter provides a brief look at the **ed** and **vi** editors and introduces the **nroff** formatter. (See Appendix 1 for a more detailed discussion of these programs and their commands.)

THE ed TEXT EDITOR

You can use the editor to create a new file or to change an existing one. To illustrate the process of creating a new file, let's create a file called "memo." UNIX uses the syntax

ed *filename*

for both creating and editing a file. To create the new file "memo," type **ed** followed by the filename "memo."

```
$ ed memo
?memo
□
```

ed responded to this command by displaying "?memo." The question mark is an error signal. Anytime you make an error in the command mode, **ed** will respond with a "?". This particular error message tells us that the filename memo was not found on the directory. We now have a chance to escape or to continue on and enter the text of our memo. To escape, enter the capital letter "Q" at the beginning of the line and press Return.

```
$ ed memo
?memo
Q
$ □
```

To continue on and enter the desired text, type the capital letter "P" and press Return. **ed** will respond with a star (*). (The star is the editor's command prompt—similar to the "$" system prompt of UNIX.) Type a lower case "a," press Return, and then type in the body of the file.

TEXT EDITING AND FORMATTING

```
$ ed memo
?memo
P
*a
Dear Reader:
How are you?
Your Author.
□
```

To inform the editor that you have finished, type a period (.) at the beginning of a line and press Return. To save the file, enter a lower case "w" and press Return. The editor will respond with the number "44," which is the number of characters (bytes) in the file. Now, to exit from the editor, type in a lowercase "q."

```
$ ed memo
?memo
P
*a
Dear Reader:
How are you?
Your Author.
.
*w
44
*q
$ □
```

The editor has two modes: the command mode and the input mode. When you enter **ed**, you are placed in the command mode automatically. A command can consist of a single letter or character followed by a Return. In the last example, the single character commands **P, a, w, .** , and **q** were used. These letters commanded the editor to:

P	turn on the command level prompt
a	append text (enter input mode)
.	return to command mode
w	write the file to the disk
q	exit from the editor
Q	abort and exit from the editor

The capital "P" provides you with the "*" prompt—visible assurance that you are in command mode. The lowercase "a" places you into input mode. The period (.) allows you to stop data input and returns you to command mode. The "w" (write) command permanently saves the file on the disk. The "q" (quit) command takes you back to the UNIX prompt, provided that you have saved your file with the "w" (write) command. With the capital "Q," you can abort the **ed** process and return to UNIX.

THE SCREEN EDITOR vi

Many UNIX systems have a screen editor **vi**, which is not a standard part of UNIX System V. A screen editor displays your document on the screen and allows you to move the cursor around and to make changes as desired. A screen editor is more like a word processor than it is like a line editor such as **ed**. A screen editor does not do formatting, but it is not difficult to produce acceptable documents using **vi**. You can accomplish the equivalent of word processing by using the **nroff** commands to format text prepared with either **vi** or **ed**.

Line editors were originally developed in the days of low speed printing terminals. Screen editors are designed for higher speed video terminals. Screen editors can have drawbacks themselves if the terminal is connected to the computer via a modem. In this case, the communications link between the computer and your terminal will be slow: 30 to 120 characters per second (cps). A terminal connected directly to the computer will have an average rate of 960 cps. Most terminals have screens that display up to 1920 characters; at a communications rate of 960, a screen is repainted in two seconds. At 30 cps, repainting the screen can take over a minute. Word processors and other screen editors are most often used on terminals that are connected directly to the computer. The **vi** (visual) editor is smart software: It adjusts the amount of the screen used for editing to match the communications rate.

TEXT EDITING AND FORMATTING

Your terminal has other characteristics, in addition to the data rate, that are used for screen operations. For example, your computer must be able to read the cursor position. It isn't hard to do, but there is, as yet, no universal way of reading the cursor position. There are some standard ways, but not all terminals conform to the same standards. To use the **vi** editor (or any other program that use full-screen operations), the terminal must be installed onto your computer's version of UNIX. There is a good chance that the terminals used with your computer are properly installed and integrated. If they are not, however, **vi** will not work properly. See your system administrator if you suspect that your terminal is improperly installed.

Creating a File Using vi

To create a new file, type **vi** and a filename. For example, the command

       $ vi demo

will create the file "demo." The editor now clears and repaints the video screen. The screen will look like the following:

```
□
~
~
~
~
~
~
"demo" [New File]
```

with the number of dashes (tildes) at the left edge of the screen determined by the communications rate. This is the window that **vi** uses for your terminal. At 30 cps, there are eight lines in the window, at 120 cps there are sixteen, and above 120 cps there are 23. The line at the bottom is the status line. The **vi** window represents the amount of your file that **vi** must display whenever the screen is repainted.

When you first enter **vi**, the cursor will be positioned to the upper left-hand corner of the display window and you will be in the **vi** command mode.

Entering Text

Press the **a** (append) key to enter the input mode. There will be no indication that you are in the input mode. Now, type in the your text. Use the Return key to get a new line. When you have finished, pressing the Escape key will return you to the command mode. Here's the procedure:

press the **a** key	enter append mode
enter the text	
press Escape	return to command mode

and a sample result:

```
Dear Reader:
     This is the vi editor.
Your Author.
□
~

~

~

"demo" [New File]
```

If you pressed the Escape key with the cursor positioned somewhere other than the beginning of a line it may have moved left one position. This is normal. The cursor will attempt to move to the last real character entered.

Saving Your File

To save your file (it is presently in a work area called a "buffer"), press the colon (:). When you press the colon (:), the last line, "demo" [New File], will be erased. The colon will appear at the beginning of the line with the cursor immediately following:

: ☐

Now, press the lowercase **w** (for the write command) and press Return. The file will be copied from the buffer to a disk file. The filename will be the name you chose when you entered **vi**. **vi** will display (in this example)

```
"demo" [New File] 4 lines, 55 characters
```

at the bottom of the screen.

Exiting the vi Editor

To exit from **vi**, you must press the colon. Then, enter a lowercase **q** and Return. That's it. You are back in UNIX. You can also combine the last commands so that you can save and exit (that is, **:wq**). Better still is **ZZ**, which accomplishes the same result (that is, save & exit) but saves keystrokes.

Follow these steps to create and save a file using the **vi** editor:

1. Enter **vi** followed by the filename (e.g., **vi demo**).
2. Press the **a** to enter the append mode.
3. Type in your document (just as if using a typewriter).
4. Press the Escape key to exit from the append mode.
5. Press the colon and the **w** to save the file (**:w**).
6. Press the colon and the **q** to exit from **vi**.

See Appendix 1 for more detailed information on using the **ed** and **vi** text editors.

FORMATTING

A formatter is a program that controls the appearance of your document when it's printed or displayed. A separate process is required for documents prepared with **ed** and **vi** because these editors do not control the format. You can, of course, perform some of the formatting by using your terminal as if it were a typewriter and inserting

blank lines and spaces where required. You'll find more formatting options in one of the UNIX formatting programs.

Two formatting programs are included as a standard part of UNIX: **nroff** and **troff**. **nroff** was designed for use with teletype terminals, but it can be used with most video terminals, line printers, and character printers that offer fixed print spacing. **troff** was designed for use with typesetting equipment, specifically, with the Graphic Systems phototypesetter. **troff** allows you to format pages similar to books with features such as print size, proportional spacing, and font selection, that is, if you're using a phototypesetter. Many modern character printers, particularly the dot matrix, laser, and ink jets printers offer most of the capabilities of a typesetting machine. In this book, we will, however, limit the discussion to the **nroff** formatter.

Formatting Commands

The layout of your document is controlled by formatting commands that you embed in your document file. The UNIX manual calls the formatting commands *requests*. These requests are inserted into your document file. The document will then consist of both the textual material and these formatting commands. A typical formatting command is shown below.

        .pl 66

This particular command sets the page length to 66 lines (11 inches).

Each command must begin with a *special character*. The special character can be either a dot (.) or an apostrophe ('). The special character must be the first character on a line. The actual command, which is two characters long (for example,**pl**), follows the special character and is followed by an optional *argument.* The argument supplies the specific parameter for the command. In our example command, the number "66" is the argument and represents the number of lines to be appear on the page. There must not be a space between the control character and the command. There must be one space between the command and the argument.

You can define your own special formatting commands. These must, however, be made up of standard formatting commands. A custom command consisting of several standard commands is called a *macro*.

Formatting Pages

The three figures below illustrate the concept of formatting. Figure 7-1 shows a standard business letter after editing, Figure 7-2 shows the same letter with the formatting commands added, and Figure 7-3 shows the letter hot off the press.

```
Softwords, Inc.
4321 Michigan Avenue
Redwood City, California
Mr. Christopher Jackson August 27, 1984
Manager, Information Systems
Low Power Laboratories
La Cucharacha, New Mexico
Dear Mr. Jackson:
We would be delighted to furnish Low Power Laboratories with
our customized word processing software. The Softword
processor is compatible with most UNIX computer systems and
can be custom installed for 375 different computer terminals
and 613 separate printers.
Prices are based on the number of terminals that can be
connected for use with the software. Quantity discounts are
provided.  Our price schedule is as follows:
QUANTITY  UNIT PRICE
1-9 $595
10-99 $495
100-999 $250
1000-9999 $125
10000-UP $ 50
We stand ready to provide assistance and training for the
installation and use of our software. A toll free trouble
hot line is staffed by our experts 24 hours a day. If you
have any further questions, feel free to call at any time.
Sincerely,
```

Figure 7-1 Edited Business Letter

```
.de MT
.sp 6
..
.de MB
.bp
..
.de IP
.sp
.ti 5
..
.wh 0 MT
.wh -6 MB
.po 15
.ll 60
.nf
.na
.ce 3
Softwords, Inc.
4321 Michigan Avenue
Redwood City, California
.sp 2
.tl 'Mr. Christopher Jackson''August 27, 1984'
Manager, Information Systems
Low Power Laboratories
La Cucharacha, New Mexico
.sp 2
Dear Mr. Jackson:
.fi
.ad
.IP
We would be delighted to furnish Low Power Laboratories
with our customized word processing software. The Softword
processor  is compatible with most UNIX computer systems
and can be custom installed for 375 different computer
terminals and 613 separate printers.
```

```
.IP
Prices are based on the number of terminals that can be
connected for use with the software. Quantity discounts are
provided.  Our price schedule is as follows:
.sp 1
.nf
.na
.ta 30C 45C
<TAB>QUANTITY<TAB>UNIT PRICE
<TAB>1-9<TAB>$595
<TAB>10-99<TAB>$495
<TAB>100-999<TAB>$250
<TAB>1000-9999<TAB>$125
<TAB>10000-UP<TAB>$ 50
.fi
.ad
.IP
We stand ready to provide assistance and training for the
installation and use of our software. A toll free
.ul
trouble hot line
is staffed by our experts 24 hours a day. If you have any
further questions, feel free to call at any time.
.sp 1
.ti 30
Sincerely,
.bp
```

Figure 7-2 Business letter with format controls

Softwords, Inc.
4321 Michigan Avenue
Redwood City, California

Mr. Christopher Jackson   August 27, 1984
Manager, Information Systems
Low Power Laboratories
La Cucharacha, New Mexico

Dear Mr. Jackson:

We would be delighted to furnish Low Power Laboratories with
our customized word processing software. The Softword processor
is compatible with most UNIX computer systems and can be custom
installed for 375 different computer terminals and 613 separate
printers.

Prices are based on the number of terminals that can be
connected used with the software. Quantity discounts are
provided. Our price schedule is as follows:

QUANTITY	UNIT PRICE
1-9	$595
10-99	$495
100-999	$250
1000-9999	$125
10000-UP	$ 50

We stand ready to provide assistance and training for the
installation and use of our software. A toll free <u>trouble hot
line</u> is staffed by our experts 24 hours a day. If you have any
further questions, feel free to call at any time.

Sincerely,

Figure 7-3 Formatted business letter

Page Layout Page layout consists primarily of the page length and the margins. When you set your page length and margins, the page layout commands will depend upon the characteristics of your printer and the size and shape of the paper you are using.

Page Length The standard page size is 8 1/2 by 11 inches. Printers are usually set to print six lines per inch. A standard page has 66 lines. The formatting command to set the page length is **pl**. To change the page length to 84 (legal size paper at 6 lines per inch), use

```
.pl 84
```

If you are using standard 11-inch paper with the standard six lines per inch you will not need to use the **pl** command. **nroff** will assume a page length of 66 lines. Such automatic settings are called *defaults*.

Left Margin Unless you specify a left margin, **nroff** will begin printing at the left edge of the paper. Use the page offset **po** command to set the left margin. The size of the page offset is given in character spaces. Use the command

```
.po 10
```

to set a 10-character wide left margin.

The size of the margin in inches is determined by your printer. Printers can typically be set to 10 (pica), 12 (elite), and 15 (little) characters per inch (cpi). The setting is usually set or changed by switches inside the printer. 10 pitch (pica) is a commonly used standard setting for computer printers. 12 pitch is more commonly used in the business office. A page offset of 10 will produce a 1-inch margin for a printer set to 10 cpi.

Right Margin The right hand margin is set by a combination of the page offset and the length of the printed line. The command for line length is **ll**. Line length is also specified in characters. The standard line length is 65 characters (6.5 inches at 10 cpi). You can set 1-inch margins for both left and right margins with

```
.po    12                 1 inch at 12 cpi
.ll    78                 6.5 inches at 12 cpi
```

(if your printer is set to 12 cpi).

When you are content with a line length of 65, the **ll** command can be omitted. **nroff** will assume a line length of 65 unless otherwise specified.

Top and Bottom Margins The **nroff** formatter does not provide either a top or a bottom margin. To obtain either (or both) you must use a macro to define your top and bottom margins. Then, you must "set a trap" that invokes the macros for the top and bottom margins.

A macro consists of the command **de** (define macro) followed by the commands that you want contained in the macro. For the top and bottom margins, define two macros called "MT" and "MB." A macro has a two character name; it's best to use uppercase letters, so that you don't inadvertently use a **nroff** command name.

To set your top margins and bottom margins to six lines from the top and bottom of the page respectively, use the following command sequence

```
.de MT              define macro named MT
.sp 6               6 blank lines
..                  end of macro
.de MB              define macro named MB
.bp                 begin new page
..                  end of macro
.wh 0 MT            use MT at beginning of page
.wh −6 MB           use MB 6 lines from bottom
```

at the beginning of your file.

The first three lines define the macro MT. MT contains one command **sp 6**. The **sp** command inserts blank lines (in this example, six blank lines) into the text. The two dots are used to define the end of the macro command list. The next macro, MB, contains the command **bp** (begin page). We call these macros with the **wh** (when) command. The **wh** command executes a named macro at a specified line number. The number following **wh** is the line number. If the line number is positive, **nroff**

counts from the top of the page. If the line number is negative, it counts from the bottom of the page. The number "0" is the beginning of the page. The number "-6" means at six lines from the bottom of the page. In this case, page refers to the length of the page (66 lines for 11 inch paper). See Appendix 1 for more discussion of **nroff** formatting commands.

Invoking nroff

Once you have entered all of the formatting commands, you are ready to use **nroff**. First, you should understand that **nroff** does not print automatically. Unless you specifically direct the formatted file to the printer, it will only be displayed on your terminal screen. Remember, if you are displaying the file on the screen, you can cause the display to pause by pressing ^S. The pause is ended by pressing ^Q.

Control - S	Pause display
Control - Q	End Pause

The general syntax is

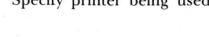

```
$ nroff options file
```

for using **nroff**. What this format means is that you can have several files printed or displayed with a single **nroff** command. The "options" available include printing only selected pages, setting the beginning page number of the document, and specifying a printer type. You should only need to specify the printer type if you are using special printer characteristics such as subscripts or superscripts. These options include:

-o[page list]	Specify pages
-n[page number]	Specify page number of first page
-s	Pause between pages to feed paper (used for single sheet feeding)
-t[printer name]	Specify printer being used

Option **-o** allows you to specify specific pages. If this option is *not* selected, the entire document will be displayed or printed. If more than one page is selected, the page list consists of the page numbers separated by commas (i.e., 5,8,9). If a range of pages is desired, the page list consists of the beginning and ending page numbers separated by a dash (i.e., 55–98.)

Option **-n** allows you to assign a starting page number to your document. For example, if you are printing the drafts of book chapters you may want to specify a starting page number of 35 for the first page of chapter 2.

Option **-s** is used when hand feeding paper into the printer. Hand feeding is often done for letterhead and special forms.

Option **-t** allows you to specify a particular printer. This option will be used only when you need the special characteristics of a particular printer. These characteristics are normally limited to half line spacing (used for subscripts and superscripts). To format and display page 2 and the 4th through the 9th pages of the file "letter" on your screen, use

```
$ nroff -o2,4-9 letter
```

and use

```
$ nroff -o2,4-9 letter | lp
```

to format and print the same pages of this file.

In this chapter, the **ed**, **vi**, and **nroff** utility programs have been outlined. The **ed** and **vi** text editors allow you to create and edit files, and the **nroff** utility program formats text for printing or display. The discussion of these programs also introduced the notions of the command line, proper syntax, and arguments.

CHAPTER EIGHT

SORTING, SEARCHING AND COMPARING FILES

UNIX provides commands for sorting, searching, and comparing the contents of files. *Sorting* allows you to arrange the contents of a file in alphabetical or numeric order. *Searching* lets you hunt for information you have stored in tables or look for key words and phrases in documents. *Comparing* files lets you look at the differences or similarities between two files.

SORTING FILES

Let's assume that you have previously created the file "distribution." This file is just a simple list of names to be used as the distribution for a letter. When the file was created, the names (data) were entered without regard for their order:

```
Cricket, James
Frog, Frederick
Aardvark, Allen
Beaver, Eager
```

the **sort** command alphabetizes this list. The command

```
$ sort distribution
```

sorts our file and displays the result on the terminal. We haven't actually changed the file "distribution." We have merely redisplayed it in a useful way. We can permanently rearrange the entries by sorting our file to a new file. The command

```
$ sort distribution > newfilename
```

will create a new file with the data in the sorted order. The > *redirects* the output of the **sort** command from the screen and creates a completely new file "newfilename" with all of the entries in alphabetical order:

```
Aardvark, Allen
Beaver, Eager
Cricket, James
Frog, Frederick
```

You can also **sort** the file and append this sorted list of names to the end of another file. For example, suppose that you have created a file named "letter," and this list contains the names of people who are to receive a copy of it (that is, the distribution list). Use the command

```
$ sort distribution >> letter
```

to **sort** the list "distribution" and add the sorted list to the end of the file "letter." The >> is used to indicate that the result of the sorting operation is to be appended to the file "letter."

You can also enter the list at the same time as you **sort** it. If you use the command

```
$ sort >> letter
```

the cursor will be placed at the beginning of the line following the command. Then, type in your list. When you have finished entering the column of names, press ^**D** to signal that you are finished. The list will be sorted automatically and will be added to the end of the file "letter."

SORTING, SEARCHING AND COMPARING FILES

The **sort** command can sort the entire line beginning with the leftmost character, or it can can sort this list by the first name. **sort** views spaces or blocks of spaces as separators between columns. So, this simple list of names is considered to be two columns. To **sort** the distribution list by the first names, use

```
$ sort +1 distribution
```

The term **+1** indicates that the first column (the last names) is to be skipped for the sorting operation. Another way to look at this is to assume that the columns are numbered from left to right and that the starting column (the leftmost) is number 0. Here is the sorted list of names:

```
Aardvark, Allen
Beaver, Eager
Frog, Frederick
Cricket, James
```

Before discussing the various options for the **sort** command, let's examine how **sort** looks at columns. This "phone book" table

```
Aardvark, Allen     23 4th Ave    Portland   OR    206-443-2231
Byers, Robert A.    3 Beach St    Carmel     CA    805-759-9242
Frog, Fred          3681 Lilly    New York   NY    914-555-8322
```

contains names, addresses, and telephone numbers. To the untutored eye, this table contains five columns. You might find it convenient to **sort** the table on the contents of any of the columns, such as city or state. You *can* do this sorting in UNIX, but you'll need to understand the rules.

Columns

sort takes an entirely different view of the "phone book" table above. This table

```
Aardvark, Allen  23    4th   Ave Portland    OR 206-443-2231
     Frog,   Fred 3681 Lilly  New     York   NY 914-555-8322
     Byers, Robert   A.    3 Beach    St Carmel    CA 805-759-9242
```

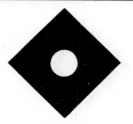

shows how **sort** considers these columns to be arranged. The five columns have become nine. Further, once you move away from the first column (column 0) the items in a column no longer have any relationship to each other.

As you can see, there is a difference between what the untutored (in UNIX) eye would consider to be the column format and what **sort** considers to be the column format. Each item that is separated by spaces from another item on the line is considered to be a separate column.

There are two simple alternatives: Set up the table so that columns align strictly or use something other than spaces as a column separator. To show how this works, let's use the colon (:) as a column separator. Here is a sample file with colons as separators:

```
Aardvark, Allen    :23 4th Ave :Portland:OR   :206-443-2231
Frog, Fred         :3681 Lilly :New York:NY   :914-555-8322
Byers, Robert A.   :3 Beach St :Carmel   :CA   :805-759-9242
```

Do *not* use a semicolon as a column separator. Do not use any character that appears in your data as a column separator.

As you can see, our table is no longer as pretty, but it has five clearly separated columns. These are referred to as columns 0 through 4. Column 0 is the leftmost column. The columns need not line up for proper sorting. An equally acceptable arrangement for **sort** is shown below.

```
Aardvark, Allen:23 4th Ave :Portland:OR:206-443-2231
Frog, Fred:3681 Lilly:New York:NY:914-555-8322
Byers, Robert A.:3 Beach St:Carmel:CA:805-759-9242
```

Use the command

```
$ sort +3t: phonebook
Byers, Robert A.  :3 Beach St :Carmel   :CA   :805-759-9242
Frog, Fred        :3681 Lilly :New York:NY   :914-555-8322
Aardvark, Allen    :23 4th Ave :Portland:OR   :206-443-2231
```

to **sort** the data so that it appears to be sorted by the contents of the state column (column 3). The **t:** added to the column number tells **sort** that the columns are separated by colons. The general syntax for the **sort** command is

SORTING, SEARCHING AND COMPARING FILES

```
sort option_list filename
```

As with most UNIX commands, the option list consists of one or more letters. Each letter is a code that represents one of the available sorting options. The available sorting options include

+#	column number to sort on
b	ignore leading blank spaces
d	use dictionary order
f	don't discriminate between uppercase and lowercase letters
m	merge two or more already sorted files
n	sort on the numeric value of a column
r	sort in reverse order
t*	use character following the t as column separator
u	discard duplicates

The option list will begin with a dash (-). If a column number is specified, the column number is prefaced by a plus sign (+). The command becomes

```
$ sort +2drut: phonebook
```

if you specify that the file is to be sorted on column 2, in reverse dictionary order with duplicates discarded, and colons are to be used for column separators.

Dictionary Order

Sorting is done in ASCII order, which is an arbitrary ordering of letters, numbers, and other symbols. ASCII ordering is standard on most computer systems. (A chart of the ASCII ordering is shown in Appendix 3.) In the ASCII system, numbers come before letters and uppercase letters come before lowercase letters. All of the printable special symbols on the keyboard are included in the ASCII sort order. With the *dictionary* ordering option added, **sort** will ignore characters other than letters and numbers. The difference between the two is illustrated by Figure 8-1.

ASCII ORDER   DICTIONARY ORDER

```
     #                    #
     $                    $
     3                    =
     :w                   ^
     =                    3
     Z                    Z
     ^                    a
     a                    :w
```

Figure 8-1 Examples of ASCII Ordering and Dictionary Ordering

Note that the colon is located in the middle of the ASCII list. In the dictionary list, it appears to have moved to the end of the list. Actually, in the dictionary list, the colon is ignored entirely. Its place in the list is set by the letter w. Symbols are first, numbers second, uppercase letters third, and lowercase letters last in dictionary ordering.

Leading Blank Spaces in Columns

A column entry may contain leading blank spaces. Blank spaces have the lowest sort value (that is, will occur first in sorting). Let's consider this simple table:

```
Frog, Freddy        301        3
Aardvark, Alvin     101        2
Gross, Very         444        1
```

This table contains the name, room, and grade for students in an elementary school. We can **sort** this list on the three-character room number without special delimiters because it is actually divided into columns. If any of the students had a middle initial, the column arrangement would be spoiled and you would have need to add special delimiters. The room number column actually begins with the first space following the students' first name. If you **sort** this list on column 2 (room number), you get the list shown below.

SORTING, SEARCHING AND COMPARING FILES

```
$ sort +2 students
Gross, Very       444       1
Frog, Freddy      301       3
Aardvark, Alvin   101       2
```

Notice how the records are actually sorted by the length of each student's complete name. There are two ways to **sort** this list properly: Ignore the leading blanks or **sort** on the numeric value of the column. The latter would not **sort** properly if there were letters in the column (for example, room A10). The command (with result also shown) for a properly sorted list is

```
$ sort +2b students
Aardvark, Alvin   101       2
Frog, Freddy      301       3
Gross, Very       444       1
```

Uppercase and Lowercase

As shown in the discussion on dictionary order, UNIX discriminates between uppercase and lowercase letters. In the student listing, the students are shown in proper alphabetical order. These names should appear in this same order whether they have capital letters or not. The command

```
$ sort -f   students
```

will sort the students regardless of capital letters. Option **f** causes **sort** to ignore case.

Sorting on Numbers

Option **n** allows you to **sort** on the numeric value of a column. Sorting normally occurs from the smallest value to the largest. Leading blank spaces are ignored when sorting with option **n**. To illustrate the use of this option, let's **sort** the room numbers for our student list. Incidentally, if an entry is non–numeric it will be placed at the beginning of the list (i.e., its numeric value is zero). The command

```
$ sort +2n students
Aardvark, Alvin    101    2
Frog, Freddy       301    3
Gross, Very        444    1
```

sorts the list of students by room.

Sorting in Reverse Order

Sorting occurs in ascending order (alphabetical, chronological, and numeric). There are any number of reasons that you might want to **sort** in the reverse (descending order). In descending order the largest numbers, the greatest dates, and the highest letters occur first. A good example of using reverse order might be to list students in order of their reading scores. To **sort** this list so that the students are arranged with the largest scores first,

Name	Room	Grade	Score
Aardvark, Alvin	101	2	87
Frog, Freddy	301	3	12
Gross, Very	444	1	95

use option **r**.

```
$ sort +4r students
Gross, Very        444    1    95
Aardvark, Alvin    101    2    87
Frog, Freddy       301    3    12
```

Sort and Merge

Suppose that you have two or more standard distribution lists. You can merge these lists into a single list for a special distribution with option **m** (merge). If the lists are already sorted, the output list will be sorted. If the lists are not sorted, the output list will be merged but not sorted. Let's merge the two sorted lists "L1" and "L2."

(Both "L1" and "L2" are disk files.) The merge and sort operation is shown as Figure 8-2.

L1	L2
Aardvark, Alvin	Boy, George
Frog, Frederick	Mandu, Cat
Mandu, Cat	

```
$ sort -m L1 L2
Aardvark, Alvin
Boy, George
Frog, Frederick
Mandu, Cat
Mandu, Cat
```

Figure 8-2 Merging the Sorted Lists L1 and L2

Getting Rid of Duplicates

Lists, particularly large ones, may contain one or more duplicate entries. Duplicate entries are likely to occur when you merge sorted lists. In our last example, the entry "Mandu, Cat" is duplicated. If the list is sorted, duplicate entries can be removed by the option **u**. Option **u** can be combined with the merge option. The list sorted and merged in Figure 8-2 is resorted and merged with the discard duplicates option added—in Figure 8-3.

L1	L2
Aardvark, Alvin	Boy, George
Frog, Frederick	Mandu, Cat
Mandu, Cat	

```
$sort -mu L1 L2
Aardvark, Alvin
Boy, George
Frog, Frederick
Mandu, Cat
```

Figure 8-3 Merging the Sorted Lists L1 and L2

This operation can take the two sorted lists, merge them together, discard the duplicates, and add the result to the end of a file. The command is

```
$ sort -mu L1 L2 >> letter
```

if the file name is "letter."

SEARCHING FILES

UNIX offers a number of commands (that is, utility programs) that allow you to search a file (or files) for a particular key word or phrase. The command most frequently used for searching is **grep** with its variations **fgrep** and **egrep**.

To understand the use of **grep** for searching files, let's search this phonebook file

```
Aardvark, Allen     23 4th Ave    Portland    OR    206-443-2231
Byers, Robert A.    3 Beach St    Carmel      CA    805-759-9242
Frog, Fred          3681 Lilly    New York    NY    914-555-8322
```

for the phone number 759-9242. How often have you needed to find the name belonging to a phone number? The command

```
$ grep "759-9242" phonebook
Byers, Robert A.  3 Beach St   Carmel    CA    805-759-9242
```

will successfully search for the person to whom the number belongs.

grep, which is an acronym for (believe it or not) *global regular expression printer*, will search for an expression and display the line or lines containing the expression. An expression can be any key word or phrase, such as our phone number. It's best to enclose the expression in either single or double quotes. The same symbol must be used on each side of the expression. The syntax for the **grep** commands is

```
$ grep option_list "expression" filenames
```

The **grep** family of commands has an extensive list of options. Those shown here are some of the most useful:

v	display all lines *not* containing the expression
c	count the lines containing the expression but do not display
l	display only filenames containing the expression

Searching Several Files

If you don't know in which file the data is contained, you can search several (or all) of your files for the information. "Fred Frog" appears in three files used in this chapter: distribution, phonebook, and students. We can search these files for "Fred" in at least two ways: listing all possible files or using a metacharacter for the filename. Either

```
$ grep "Frog, Fred" distribution phonebook students
```

or

```
$ grep "Frog, Fred" *
```

will produce this display:

```
$ grep "Frog, Fred" *
distribution: Frog, Frederick
phonebook: Frog, Fred    3681 Lilly    New York    NY    914-555-8322
students: Frog, Freddy    301    3    12
```

Notice that each displayed line begins with the filename it came from. The searching operation is fastest when you are searching named files; so, it is faster not to use the wildcard (*). When you name the files, you are doing part of the work of **grep**.

Deleting Lines of Text with grep

Suppose Fred has gone away. You want to delete him from the records. You could, of course, use the text editor and delete the lines. Another way to accomplish this task is to use **grep** with option **v**. Use **grep** to locate the name. Option **v** will display all lines *not* containing Fred. Send the output to a file ("newphones") instead of the screen with the > (the redirect command) symbol. Then, delete the file "phonebook" using the **rm** command and rename "newphones" to "phonebook" using the **mv** command:

```
$ grep -v "Frog, Fred" phonebook > newphones
$ rm phonebook
$ mv newphones phonebook
$ □
```

The file "phonebook" will no longer contain an entry for "Fred Frog."

Searching with Wildcards

There are a number of symbols that can be used to help you with your search. These symbols are

.	(dot) substitute for any character
*	(star) substitute for a group of characters
^	(caret) beginning of the line
$	(dollar sign) end of the line
[ ]	(square brackets) ranges of characters

Metacharacters cannot be used with **fgrep**, but they can be used with both **grep** and **egrep**.

The Dot The dot (.) can be used as a wildcard substitute for any character. You may want to search for the name "Byers" but aren't sure whether it is spelled with an "a" or an "e." Use the command

```
$ grep "By.rs" phonebook
```

and the display will show all the lines that contain "By" followed by any character and followed, in turn, by "rs." Use the dot for any particular character of which you are unsure.

Square brackets Brackets are used to limit wildcard substitution to specify characters. In the example above, although it is unlikely, you could have also found any of the following:

By#rs   By2rs   By=rs

You knew, however, that the unknown character was lowercase. Use the square brackets to tell **grep**. The characters appearing in the brackets are the only acceptable wildcards. In the "By.rs" example, the wildcard had to be a vowel. So, change the search command to

```
$ grep "By[aeiou]rs"
```

You can also use the brackets to specify ranges of characters:

[A-Z]   indicates all uppercase letters
[a-z]   indicates all lowercase letters
[0-9]   indicates all numeric digits

You should be aware that when you specify digits as a wildcard you are not specifying them as numbers but as characters. The specification [100-999] does not broaden the

range to any number between 100 and 999 but simply limits one character to the range 0 to 9.

The Star (*) can also be used as a wildcard substitute within **grep**. However, you need to be a little wary here. The star is used differently within the **grep** expression and the list of files to be searched.

To search all files beginning with the letter "B" for the text pattern "dogs and cats" the command would look like:

```
$ grep "dogs and cats" B*
```

In this case, UNIX is evaluating your use of the star. The star is a substitute for any character sequence.

grep, however, attaches a different meaning to the star when it is used as a wildcard within a search pattern. In the **grep** context, the star means any sequence of one or more of the characters preceding the star. B* indicates any sequence of zero or more B's—as opposed to the above usage of any filename beginning with a B. "aB*c" will match ac, abc, abbc, abbbc, and ab.....bc.

The **grep** search equivalent to the use of B* for a filename search is B.* (a dot followed by a star). Taken literally, this means look for a "B" followed by zero or more wildcard (dot) characters.

```
$ grep "B.*" B*
```

Beginning of a Line To specify that the desired search pattern is at the beginning of a line use the caret (^) before the pattern. For example, suppose there is a fellow named "Carmel" in our phonebook. Searching for Mr. Carmel will turn up both his record and all the records of people who live in Carmel. Because the person's name begins the line, the command

```
$ grep "^Carmel" phonebook
```

can conduct the search.

End of a Line To specify that a desired search pattern is at the end of a line, use the dollar sign ($) after the pattern. For example, suppose that you want to search for the four-digit sequence "9242" in the phonebook file. It's always possible that this sequence will show up as an address. The command

```
$ grep "9242$" phonebook
```

will indicate that it is at the end of a line.

Uppercase and Lowercase

What should you do if you don't know the exact representation in uppercase and lowercase. For example, "Carmel" might be spelled as "Carmel," "carmel," or "CARMEL." If you are completely unsure, you can use square brackets ([ ]) to indicate groups of characters. The command

```
$ grep "[cC][aA][rR][mM][eE][lL]"   phonebook
```

will display all lines containing any uppercase and lowercase variation of the letters in "Carmel."

FAST SEARCHES (fgrep)

The utility program (that is, command) **fgrep** is designed to search files rapidly. You cannot use wildcards or metacharacters in the search pattern when using **fgrep**. **fgrep** searches a file for the exact expression you have entered. Otherwise, it operates exactly the same way as does **grep**. Although you cannot use metacharacters in the search pattern, you can use them to identify the files to be searched.

EXTENDED GREP (egrep)

You can specify searching alternatives with **egrep.** So, you can search the files for several items at once. Use the command

```
$ egrep "Carmel|New York" phonebook
Byers, Robert A.  3 Beach St  Carmel    CA  805-759-9242
Frog, Fred        3681 Lilly  New York  NY  914-555-8322
```

if you want to see all of the lines that contain either "Carmel" or "New York" in our phonebook file. You can combine alternatives with other parts of a search pattern by enclosing the alternatives within parentheses. Use this file of students sorted by score:

Name	Room	Grade	Score
Gross, Very	444	1	95
Aardvark, Alvin	101	2	87
Frog, Freddy	301	3	12

Assume there are several "Frogs" in the school. You don't know the first name of M. Frog but you do know that the desired "Frog" is in either room 715 or 301. The proper command would be

```
$ egrep "Frog.* (715 | 301)" students
Frog, Freddy       301       3       12
```

COMPARING FILES

There can be any number of reasons when you might want to know the differences (if any) between two files. Using the computer to help you compare is more valuable if the files are large. The **diff** command will tell you which lines have changed, which have been added, and which have been deleted. Using the **diff** command, let's compare the two disk files, "oldfile" and "newfile."

SORTING, SEARCHING AND COMPARING FILES

oldfile	newfile
Aardvark, Allen	Aardvark, Al
Beaver, Eager	Beaver, Eager
Frog, Fred	Milton, John
Milton, John	Shakespear, W
Shakespear, W	Whitman, Walt

A visual inspection of these files shows you that the first entry has been changed, "Fred Frog" has been deleted and "Walt Whitman" has been added. This is essentially what you will learn from using the **diff** command. The order of the filenames is important. Usually you will enter the old file name first and the new file name last.

The form of the **diff** command is

```
$ diff oldfile  newfile
1c1
<Aardvark, Allen
---
>Aardvark, Al
3d2
<Frog, Fred
5a5
>Whitman, Walt
```

The output from **diff** can be decoded in the following way: The "1c1" indicates that **diff** recognized that line 1 had been changed. This can be read as line 1 has been changed and is still line 1. The next three lines indicate the way it was and the way it is. The arrows indicate which file the following text came from. The ">" means that it came from the newfile. The "<" means that it came from the old file.

The message "3d2" tells us that line 3 of oldfile has been deleted. The following line "<Frog, Fred" is the deleted line. The message "5a5" means that "Walt Whitman" was added as line 5 in the old file. The second "5" shows us that it is also line 5 in the new file. The following line ">Whitman, Walt" is the line that has been added. All of this provides enough information to reconstruct the original file by working from the change summary provided by **diff**. Remember that the messages

depend upon your entering the filenames in the correct order. **diff** doesn't know which file was created first.

There are two principal options that can be used with **diff**: option **e**, which produces an output that can be used directly with the text editor **ed** , and option **b**, which ignores changes in the spacing between words.

WHAT'S COMMON

Another way to compare files is to look for what's common between the two. For example, you might want to compare two lists to check for common entries. The **comm** command will compare two files and tell you what is common. If you are comparing lists, you will want to **sort** the lists before you make the comparison. Comparing the same two files with **comm** that were compared with **diff** shows the use of the **comm** command.

oldfile	newfile
Aardvark, Allen	Aardvark, Al
Beaver, Eager	Beaver, Eager
Frog, Fred	Milton, John
Milton, John	Shakespear, W
Shakespear, W	Whitman, Walt

The comparison is accomplished by the command

```
$ comm oldfile newfile
Aardvark, Allen
        Aardvark, Al
                Beaver, Eager
Frog, Fred
                Milton, John
                Shakespear, W
        Whitman, Walt
```

Notice that there are three overlapping columns, which together display all of the data from both files. They are each indented eight spaces from the left edge of the screen. The first column contains the lines that are only in "oldfile." The second column contains only those items which are in "newfile." The third column contains the items that are common to both files. As you can tell, this format is hard to read. It is even harder to read when the lines cover most of the screen. Fortunately, you can limit the display to the common lines. The three columns above are numbered 1, 2, and 3. To view only column 3 (the common items), you must suppress columns 1 and 2 with the command

```
$ comm -12 oldfile newfile
Beaver, Eager
Milton, John
Shakespear, W
```

Now, only the items from column 3 are displayed. They have also been formatted so that they now appear at the left margin of the screen.

This chapter has shown the range of commands (utility programs) that UNIX provides to sort, search, and compare files. The command **sort** can be used in combination with various parameters to organize and format output. The commands **grep**, **fgrep**, and **egrep** will search for an expression and display the line or lines containing the expression. You can compare files with either **diff** or **comm**. **diff** will display differences between two files and **comm** will display what's common between them.

CHAPTER NINE

PIPES, TEES, AND FILTERS

Some terms that you may encounter while you are becoming familiar with UNIX include: pipes, tees, filters, standard input and output, redirection, foreground, and background. These terms all involve simple and familiar concepts.

STANDARD INPUT and STANDARD OUTPUT

Most of you will use your UNIX computer with a video terminal and its keyboard. In UNIX jargon, these ordinary devices are called the standard output and the standard input. Your terminal is the *standard output* and the keyboard is the *standard input*. These terms are used repeatedly in the UNIX manual. If you substitute terminal and keyboard for these UNIX terms when you are reading the manual, you won't be confused.

REDIRECTION

Most of the UNIX display commands, such as **ls**, **cat**, and **sort**, send their output to the terminal. Hence the term standard output. However, you can choose to have the display sent to a disk file instead of the screen by *redirecting* the output. For example,

the **ls** command will display the names of disk files on your computer terminal. Use the command

$ls > directory

to have the **ls** command send the display to a disk file named "directory." The greater than symbol (>) indicates that the output of the command is to be sent to the file named "directory." Anything that can be displayed on the screen as the result of a command can also be written to a disk file. If the disk file does not already exist, it will be created. If it already exists, it will be overwritten.

One of the most common uses of redirection is to enter data directly from the keyboard into a disk file with the **cat** or **sort** commands. In the example below, after the command is entered, the cursor is placed on the line immediately below the UNIX prompt. Data can then be entered directly from the keyboard. To indicate that you have finished, press the Control key and the D key (**^D**) at the same time.

```
$ cat > notes
This data gets entered directly into the
disk file notes.
When finished entering data, press Control and D.
^D
```

A variation of redirection allows you to add data to the end of an existing file. To do this use the greater than symbol twice (>>).

$ ls >> directory

In this example, the output of the **ls** command will be added to the end of the file "directory." Again, if the disk file does not already exist, it will be created.

One common use of this variation of redirection is to add a distribution list to the end of a memo. For example, suppose that you already have a disk file "memo.1234" that you have created with a word processing program. You want to add a sorted distribution list to the end of this memo.

PIPES, TEES, AND FILTERS

```
$ sort >> memo.1234
    bob
    carol
    ted
    alice
    ^D
```

The list that you enter from the keyboard is sorted and added to the end of the existing disk file "memo.1234." As usual, **^D** is used to terminate data entry.

It is also possible to substitute a disk file for the keyboard as the input for a command. This redirection of the standard input is not as generally useful as redirecting the output. In fact, there are few practical uses of this feature. Most UNIX commands such as **cat** and **sort** can make direct use of disk files without redirecting the input. Two commands that can make practical use of this feature are **mail** and **write**. Neither of these commands are constructed to make direct use of disk files. Let's suppose that you have prepared a report or a memo using a word processor and want to send it to a number of other users via the UNIX electronic mail system. Our sample file name is "memo.1234." We can send this memo to our friends bob, carol, ted, and alice with

$ **mail bob carol ted alice < memo.1234**

Note that the input redirection symbol is the less than symbol (<). Another practical use for redirection is with the **write** command. When you use this command, the recipient usually gets to see you type on his or her screen—one line at a time. If you use this command

$ **write bob < notetobob**

you can prepare the message that you want to transmit ahead of time and then send it all at once.

It is possible to combine input redirection with output redirection in the same command. I can't, however, think of a practical example where combining the two

would be useful. On the bad side, if you transpose the input and output redirection symbols, you could destroy your files. In short, don't use input and output redirection together.

PIPES

Pipes provide you with another way to redirect. They redirect the output of a command so that it becomes the input for a second command. Let's suppose that you want a printed copy of our disk directory. You could do this by redirecting the output of the **ls** command to the disk file "directory" and then by printing the content of "directory" with the **lp** command:

```
$ ls > directory
$ lp directory
```

With a *pipe*, you can connect the two commands—and bypass the need for the disk file "directory." With the command

```
$ ls | lp
```

you pipe the output of the **ls** command into the **lp** command. The vertical bar (|) is the symbol for a pipe. Routing the output of a command to the printer rather than the terminal is a common use of piping.

You can use more than one pipe in a command. For example, suppose that you wanted a printed copy of your directory and that you also wanted this copy printed in four columns instead of the standard single column provided by the **ls** command. You could use the following sequence of commands to accomplish the desired result.

```
$ ls > directory
$ pr -4 directory > dirprint
$ lp dirprint
$ rm directory, dirprint
```

The same result can be achieved in a simpler way with pipes. This same sequence of commands can be accomplished on the single command line

$ ls | pr -4 | lp

which uses two pipes. The output of the **ls** command is piped into the **pr** command. The formatted output of the **pr** command becomes the input for the **lp** command. You haven't had to use intermediate disk files and what you are doing is easier to understand. This one command line has replaced the four command lines in the original example.

FILTERS

Some UNIX commands may appear to change or transform the input in some predictable way. These commands are sometimes referred to as *filters*. Examples of the filter commands are **sort**, **grep**, and **pr**. When we place these commands in the pipelines, they help to shape the output for us. The **pr** command was used as a filter to format the output of the **ls** command in the last example.

$ ls | pr -4 | lp

TEES

Use **tee**s to split the output of a process and send it to both the standard output (the terminal) and a disk file at the same time. You can use the command to view the result of a process like **sort**, as well as save the result to a file. The command

$ sort distribution | tee distlist

sorts the file "distribution" and saves the result in the file "distlist." At the same time, the sorted file is displayed on the terminal.

You can use **tee**s in pipelines to help you troubleshoot a process that isn't going quite right. At each joint of your pipeline, insert a **tee**. The process won't be displayed on your terminal (the output is redirected to the next command in the pipeline), but

you'll have a copy of what goes on at each stage of the process. Looking at these records will help you track down what you are doing wrong. In this example command,

```
$ ls | tee savedir | pr -4 | tee saveoutput | lp
```

the output of the **ls** command is routed to the **pr** command and to the disk file "savedir." Similarly, the output of the **pr** command is routed to the **lp** command and to the disk file "saveoutput."

FOREGROUND and BACKGROUND

UNIX is a multi-tasking system. Multi-tasking allows you to do two or more things at the same time. For example, suppose that you want to sort a large database and then format the output for a special report. At the same time, you want to prepare a memo and you don't want to wait until the report has finished. UNIX will let you do both at the same time. The memo that you are working on is in the *foreground*. The sorting process is in the *background*.

Processes (commands) normally run in the foreground. All that you have to do to run a command in the background is to tack on an *ampersand* (&) to the end of the command. For example, use the command

```
$ sort database > sortfile &
2001
```

to sort the file "database" in the background. Note that the output of the **sort** command is redirected to the file "sortfile." If you do not do this, the result of the **sort** command is displayed on the screen—even though it is a background task.

When you identify a command as being run in the background, UNIX will return a number and then provide you a prompt. The command hasn't finished; you are in the foreground and can go about your business while the background process runs. The number is an identification number for your background process. You can check on the status of the process by using the **ps** (process status) command. The **ps** command will display the current status of all processes running in your part of the computer.

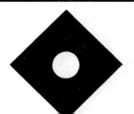

If you should change your mind about the background process, you can stop the process at any time with the **kill** command. The command

```
$ kill 2001
```

will **kill** the **sort** command from the example above.

Whenever you run a process (and you can run more than one at a time), you are using more of your computers CPU power. If everyone using the computer does the same thing, the computer will appear to run slower (and slower and slower). If everyone cooperates, you can conspire to bring even very large computers to their knees. At that point, working with the machine can be like wading through molasses. Press a key and wait for it to appear on your terminal screen. Usually, when you run a process in the background, you aren't in any hurry for it to finish. When this is the case, begin your command with **nice**, which assigns a low priority to the background task and keeps it from slowing down the foreground tasks. To run a command in the **nice** mode, you pair the command with the command **nice** as shown below. The command line

```
$ nice sort database > sortfile &
```

uses **nice** to run the **sort** command as a low priority background task.

As you have seen, UNIX uses specific terms to refer to a variety of items. Standard input is usually the keyboard. Standard output is the terminal. Redirection means to substitute a disk file for your keyboard or your terminal. Pipes (|) allow you to use the output of a command as the input for another command. With tees, you can send the output of a command to two places—your terminal screen *and* a disk file. A filter is a command that transforms a file (or your keyboard input) in some way. Foreground processing is the normal command processing that occurs in response to keyboard commands. Background processing allows you to tell the computer to perform some tasks in a way that leaves you free to use the keyboard to continue with your work. You can review the status of background tasks with the **ps** command. You can stop a background task at any time with the **kill** command. You can assign your background task as a low priority item by using the **nice** command.

CHAPTER TEN

SHELLS

There are two parts to UNIX: the kernal and the shell. The *kernel* is the core of the UNIX operating system, the part that actually does the work of program execution. The *shell* is the part of UNIX on the display, the part with which you work. The shell accepts your commands and displays its response. You use the shell to communicate with the kernal.

The shell is, in fact, just another UNIX utility program. The shell program, **sh**, is called automatically when you enter UNIX. There are actually several shell programs available. A particular UNIX computer may offer you a choice of several of these shells.

The standard shell program used with UNIX is the Bourne shell. Another common shell program is the C shell. The C shell is often standard on computers that use the Berkeley version of UNIX. New shell programs from a variety of sources will offer users the convenience of menu-driven operation.

So far in this book you have learned how to use the UNIX utility programs as commands to accomplish tasks. The Bourne and C shells provide additional commands, called the *shell commands*, that you can use to make working with UNIX simpler and more convenient. There are differences between the two shells. This book uses the Bourne shell for its examples. (This shell is supported by AT&T and we can expect that it will be around for some time to come.)

With the shell commands in both the Bourne and C shells, you can write short programs called *shell scripts*. Shell scripts allow you to customize UNIX and make it more convenient to use.

For example, the **ls** command produces (on most UNIX systems) an alphabetical list of the filenames in a directory. The filenames are usually displayed with one name on each line of the screen. If you have more than 24 filenames (the number of lines on your screen), the beginning of the list will flash by and disappear off the screen before you can read it. You can have the filenames displayed in several columns by *piping* the **ls** command into the **pr** command. The combined command

$$\text{\$ ls | pr -5 -l24 -w78}$$

will display the file names in five columns on your screen, which substantially increases the number of filenames that can appear on a single screen. The display uses all 24 lines with 78 spaces per line. Unfortunately, although this command provides a more convenient and useful display of filenames, it is a bother to use. With the shell commands, you can turn this command line into an easy-to-use command that we will call **DIR** (for **DIR**ectory).

YOUR OWN VERSION OF ls

Entering this command line into a text file creates a *shell script*. You can create the file named "DIR" with the **cat** command. Remember, once you have entered the command line, use ^D to exit from **cat** and to save the file. The sequence looks like this:

```
$ cat > DIR
ls | pr -5 -l24 -w78
^D
```

Use the **sh** command followed by the name of the shell script

```
$ sh DIR
```

to execute this shell script. To take one further step and make **DIR** into a stand-alone command that you can execute without the need for the **sh** command, you must indicate to the shell that "DIR" is an executable file. Use the **chmod** (see Chapter 6) to change the access privileges and make this file executable. The command

```
$ chmod ugo+x DIR
```

will change all three groups of access privilege (user, group, other) to be executable, in addition to whatever settings previously existed. From this point on, you can use **DIR** as a command whenever you want the custom directory display. The custom directory command

```
$ DIR
```

will always display the entire directory. Suppose that you would like only a subset of the directory displayed. The **ls** command will allow you to view the names of a subset of the directory. For example, you can use

```
$ ls M*
```

to view the names of files that begin with a capital "M." The shell can provide the directory command **DIR** with this same capability. Each item that follows a command is an argument. Our last example had one argument: M*. The command

```
$ ls framework dbase
```

has two arguments: framework and dbase. The custom directory command can accept up to nine arguments—if you add the digits 1 through 9 to the command as shown below. Each of the digits must be used with the dollar sign ($).

```
$ cat > DIR
ls $1 $2 $3 $4 $5 $6 $7 $8 $9 | pr -5 -l24 -w78
^D
```

You can also replace all the $ signs with **$*** and save some typing. The symbols such as "$1" are called *positional variables*. Each is associated with an argument. The first positional variable, "$1," is associated with the first argument. The second, "$2," is associated with the second argument, and so on. If there are fewer arguments than there are variables the empty variables are automatically discarded and ignored. If there are more arguments than there are variables the extra arguments are ignored.

Now, set the access permissions on the rewritten **DIR** command so that it becomes an executable command. Use the command

```
$ chmod ugo=rx DIR
```

and you remove the write permission (if it existed) for everyone. The file is left as readable in addition to being executable. The file must be readable to be executed. Because the write permissions have been removed, you must restore them to change the file. Removing the write permissions makes it difficult to accidentally erase the file. You can improve the custom directory command further by making it possible to use either uppercase (**DIR**) or lowercase (**dir**). Use the **ln** (link) command:

```
$ ln DIR dir
```

This command creates a link from the filename "dir" to the filename "DIR." You can now use either **DIR** or **dir** for the custom directory command.

DIR is the command used to display directory filenames on most personal computers, including on the IBM PC. If you learned to use the operating system commands of the IBM Personal Computer (PC-DOS), you may feel more comfortable with PC-DOS. You can, if you wish, write shell scripts in UNIX that create a set of commands, such as the custom **DIR**, that will make UNIX appear to be identical to PC-DOS for most of your day-to-day activities. You can even choose to change the UNIX prompt from the dollar sign ($) to anything else. For example, you can change the prompt to

```
C>
```

which is the prompt most often seen on hard disk versions of personal computers.

SHELLS

Shell scripts can capture complicated commands or sequences of commands into a single command. This makes it easier and more efficient to work with the computer—and also reduces the chance for error.

CHAPTER ELEVEN

SHELL SCRIPTS

The last chapter discussed how shell scripts can be used to customize UNIX and make it more convenient for you to use. This chapter explores the special shell commands and demonstrates ways in which they can be applied. Most of us learn more readily if new information is presented in practice. In this chapter, you will learn the shell commands and their uses while writing shell scripts that make UNIX friendlier and easier to use.

There are those who feel that UNIX is not as friendly or forgiving as it could be. For example, if you use the **cat** command and forget to add the filename you want displayed, the cursor will be positioned just below the word "cat" waiting for you to enter text and whatever you might enter won't be saved. And you do have to enter a ^D to escape back to the shell.

```
$ cat
^D
```

PC-DOS, the operating system used on the IBM Personal Computer, has a command called TYPE that displays the contents of a file. In that system, if you forget to add the

CHAPTER ELEVEN

filename, the message "invalid number of parameters" is displayed. Such a message isn't a major increase in friendliness—but it is a start.

To introduce the command TYPE into the UNIX system, use the **cat** command (or any of the editors) to create the basic command file "TYPE."

```
$ cat TYPE
cat $1
^D
```

The new command **TYPE** is more restrictive than **cat** and has all of its liabilities. In order to get **TYPE** to recognize when the filename is forgotten and to display an error message to tell us what's wrong, you must add to the command words to the effect

> if there is no filename
> display "you forgot the filename"
> otherwise display the file contents

The shell provides us with a close equivalent of the above statement—in the somewhat stilted English of the shell, but it's understandable when you know the jargon. Let's take a closer look at the above statement. It can be generalized as

> if a condition is true
> then take one action
> otherwise take another action

This pattern of reasoning is common in everyday life. If it looks like rain, take an umbrella. If the gas gauge shows low, buy gas. One evaluates a condition, such as the weather or the gas gauge, and then takes an action that depends on the evaluation. Often, the alternative action is implicitly take no action.

To solve the **TYPE** problem, you must find a way for the procedure to evaluate whether or not a filename has been entered. Remember, if we don't enter one, there is no positional variable $1. To determine the number of arguments, use the **test** command. **test** is a standard UNIX utility program. The first line is

```
if test $# -eq 0
```

with the # representing the number of arguments that have been entered after the word "TYPE." If we haven't entered any, "$#" will be zero and the condition (**test $# -eq 0**) will be true. Then, define what action is to take place, which is "display the error message." Use

```
then echo "you forgot the filename"
```

Next, define the alternative action. In this case, it is

```
else cat $1
```

Finally, unlike in ordinary English, you must signal when you have reached the end of the actions. In UNIX, you spell the action backwards: "if" backwards is "fi." Put all of these lines together and the command for displaying the contents of a file becomes

```
if test $# -eq 0
then echo "you forgot the filename"
else cat $1
fi
```

The term "-eq" in the condition means "equal." In the shell, it is called a *primitive*. UNIX has several primitives that can be used for comparing two numbers; they are

-eq	equal
-ne	not equal
-gt	greater than
-lt	less than
-ge	greater than or equal to
-le	less than or equal to

Let's make the new **TYPE** command friendly. And in the process, we can learn more about using the shell. Let's change **TYPE** so that it ignores any following arguments

and asks us for the name of the file that is to be displayed. Now, we need to consider what happens if we don't enter any filename, if the filename doesn't exist, and if it does exist but is a directory. We can write out what we need to do as

> display "Enter the name of the file"
> > enter the filename
>
> if no filename
> > then escape
>
> if filename not a file
> > then display "couldn't find the file"
> > > escape
>
> if filename is a directory
> > then display "file is a directory"
> > > escape
>
> if file exists
> > then display the file

This series translates into the specific set of commands:

```
echo "Enter the name of the file to be displayed"
    read FILE
if test -z "$FILE"
    then exit
fi
if test ! -s "$FILE"
    then echo "sorry - couldn't find the file"
        exit
fi
if test ! -f "$FILE"
    then echo "the file is a directory"
        exit
fi
cat $FILE
```

This set introduces some new commands. **read** FILE halts the procedure's execution while the file name is entered. The filename is stored in the temporary location "FILE." "FILE" is the name of the location. "FILE" could have been called almost anything. "FILE" is a variable.

In the next series of tests, use primitives to evaluate character strings. The primitive **-z** is used to determine whether a filename is entered. If no filename was entered (i.e., Return was pressed), nothing is stored in the variable "FILE." Note that the variable name is prefaced with a dollar sign ($) and is enclosed in double quotes. Use the **exit** command to escape from the procedure; you will be returned to the UNIX prompt.

Next, test to see whether the filename entered is valid. The primitive **-s** evaluates whether or not the item stored in "FILE" is an actual filename. In this case, turning the logic around will make the condition true when the filename is not in the directory. The exclamation mark (!) reverses the logic. The command line

```
if test ! -s "$FILE"
```

is read by UNIX as: If the name stored in the variable file is *not* the name of a disk file.

If you reach the following test, you know that the name is a valid filename. You don't know, however, whether it is a directory name or not. This test (the **-f**) determines whether or not the name entered is for a directory. Again, turn the test around with the exclamation mark. The command line

```
if test ! -f "$FILE"
```

is read as: If the name stored in the variable "FILE" is *not* an ordinary file (i.e., it is a directory).

Notice that the last two **if**s showed the **exit** command on a line by itself. That's okay. The exit belongs to the line **then**. You can have as many commands within an **if** as you like. Each command should be on a separate line as in this example. You can put more than one command on a line. If there is to be more than one command on a line, the commands must be separated by semicolons (;), as shown below:

```
then echo "The file is a directory" ; exit
```

The punch line **cat** $FILE is not inside of an **if**. It doesn't need to be. The previous **if**s have take care of screening out all of the bad things that can happen—which means that the order in which the **if**s appear is important. Look at the English equivalent and think through the logic.

The last example used three additional primitives. There are several primitives available in UNIX for evaluating character strings. (Filenames and other sequences of characters are called "character strings.") These primitives evaluate the character string according to specific rules and return a value of true or false to the test command.

PRIMITIVES FOR EVALUATING CHARACTER STRINGS

Primitive	Evaluates as true when
-z	Character string is empty (zero length)
-n	Character string is not empty
-s	The string is the name of a disk file
-f	The string is an ordinary disk file
-d	The string is a directory
-r	The string is the name of a readable disk file
-w	The string is the name of a writeable disk file

To give you practice creating your own commands with the shell, let's create three more commands: **ERASE**, **RENAME**, and **COPY**. These commands, as you might guess, *erase* a file, *rename* a file, and *copy* a file. They are going to operate similarly to the **TYPE** command.

ERASE

The plain English equivalent of the new **ERASE** command is shown below. Examples like this one are sometimes referred to as pseudo-code because they take the form of the actual procedure but don't use the detail commands.

```
display "Enter the name of the file"
    enter the filename
if no filename
    then escape
if filename not a file
    then display "couldn't find the file"
        escape
if filename is a directory
    then display "file is a directory"
        escape
if file exists
    then delete (erase) it
```

This pseudo-code translates into the specific set of UNIX commands below:

```
echo "Enter the name of the file to be erased"
    read FILE
if test -z "$FILE"
    then exit
fi
if test ! -s "$FILE"
    then echo "sorry - couldn't find $FILE"
        exit
fi
if test ! -f "$FILE"
    then echo "$FILE is a directory"
        exit
fi
rm $FILE
```

Notice how similar this command is to the **TYPE** command. The difference is primarily in the messages that are presented with the **echo** command. Notice that we included "**$FILE**" within the message. When the message is displayed, the contents of "**$FILE**"

will be displayed. The other difference, of course, is that we have used the **rm** (remove) command to erase the file.

RENAME

The **RENAME** command is somewhat more complex than either the **TYPE** or **ERASE** commands. The increased complexity becomes necessary because you have to evaluate two file names: the current name and the desired name. The desired name cannot be the name of an existing file. If you change your mind and enter a Return as the new filename, the command will abort.

```
display "Enter the name of the file"
    enter the filename
if no filename
    then escape
if filename not a file
    then display "couldn't find the file"
            escape
if filename is a directory
    then display "file is a directory"
            escape

display "Enter the new filename"
    enter the new filename
if filename
    and the new name doesn't already exist
        rename the file to the new filename
```

This series translates into the set of commands:

```
echo "Enter the name of the file to be renamed"
    read FILE
if test -z "$FILE"
    then exit
```

```
fi
if test ! -s "$FILE"
    then echo "sorry - couldn't find the file"
        exit
fi
if test ! -f "$FILE"
    then echo "the file is a directory"
        exit
fi

echo "Enter the new name for $FILE"
    read NEWNAME
if test ! -z "$NEWNAME"
    then if test ! -s "$ NEWNAME"
            then mv $FILE $NEWNAME
        fi
fi
```

If you look at this procedure carefully, you will see that it is an enlarged version of the previous commands. The new feature is that you can contain **if**s within **if**s. Each **if** must be terminated by a **fi**.

COPY

The **COPY** command is even more complex than the **RENAME** command. The first part of the command is similar to the **RENAME** command, but the case arises where the filename to be copied already exists and you still want to make the copy.

```
    display "Enter the name of the file to be copied"
        enter the filename
    if no filename
        then escape
```

```
if filename not a file
    then display "couldn't find the file"
        escape
if filename is a directory
    then display "file is a directory"
        escape

display "Enter the name of the new file"
    enter the new filename
if no new filename
    escape
if the new name already exists and it doesn't belong to a directory
        display "do you want to overwrite the file"
            enter the answer
        if the answer is yes
            copy the file
```

which translates into the set of commands:

```
echo "Enter the name of the file to be copied"
    read FILE
if test -z "$FILE"
    then exit
fi
if test ! -s "$FILE"
    then echo "sorry - couldn't find the file"
        exit
fi
if test ! -f "$FILE"
    then echo "the file is a directory"
        exit
fi

echo "Enter the file name for the copy of $FILE"
```

```
        read NEWFILE
if test -z "$NEWFILE"
    then exit
fi
if test -s "$NEWFILE"
    then if test ! -f "$NEWFILE"
        then echo "the file is a directory"
            exit
        else echo "$NEWFILE exists - overwrite Y/N ?"
        read OVERWRITE
        if test "$OVERWRITE" != "Y"
            then exit
        fi
    fi
fi
cp $FILE $NEWFILE
```

In the last set of **ifs**, you test to see whether the filename already exists. If it does exist, you have two possibilities: It can be an ordinary file or it can be a directory. If it is a directory, you want to escape. If it's an ordinary file, ask if the file is to be overwritten. If the answer to the question is *not* a capital "Y," escape. The symbol "=" indicates that the test is to see whether both items are the same. The symbol "!=" indicates that the test looks to see whether both items are different.

MENUS

You can also use the shell commands to set up menus. Menus can simplify the use of a computer. Activities done only occasionally can be reliably performed. Let's set up a menu of the five new commands. Here's the screen:

```
1 - Display the disk directory
2 - Display contents of a file
3 - Copy a file
4 - Erase a file
5 - Rename a file
6 - Exit back to UNIX
Enter the Number for Your Selection
        Then press the Return Key
□
```

First, enter this menu as a text file. Use **cat**, **ed**, or **vi** to create it. Use blank lines and spaces to format the screen into a centered display. The file should have 23 lines (including blanks)— so that the cursor will end up on line 24 when the file is used. Name the file "TEXT."

Next, write a procedure that will display this screen and select the proper command when a number is entered. The following pseudo-code

```
display the menu
accept a selection
execute the command corresponding to the selection
```

translates into the command set:

```
pr -l24 -w78  TEXT
read CHOICE
case "$CHOICE" in
     1) DIR ;;
     2) TYPE ;;
     3) COPY ;;
     4) ERASE ;;
     5) RENAME ;;
     6) exit ;;
esac
```

esac (case spelled backwards) closes the **case** command. In this procedure, the **pr** command is used to display the menu file "TEXT" on the screen. When the file is displayed, the cursor will be positioned at the lower left corner of the screen waiting for the selection. The selection is stored at the memory location named "CHOICE."

Next, use the **case** command to compare the entry with the possible actions. The comparison is made with the number to the left of the right parenthesis. The parenthesis separates the choices from the actions. The choices could have been the letters "a" through "f":

```
case  "$CHOICE"  in
      a)  DIR  ;;
      b)  TYPE  ;;
      c)  COPY  ;;
      d)  ERASE  ;;
      e)  RENAME  ;;
      f)  exit  ;;
esac
```

Two semicolons are used to identify the end of each action. Each case selection is equivalent to an **if**. Specifically, the case is similar to

```
if  "$CHOICE"  =  "1"
    then DIR
fi
if  "$CHOICE"  =  "2"
    then TYPE
fi
```

and so on. Using **case** requires less typing than using **if**, and the result is easier to read.

This shell script MENU accepts one choice and then stops. The menu needs to reselect itself automatically. There are two ways to do this in the shell: **while** and **until**. **while** causes a procedure to repeat as long as a condition is true. **until** repeats the procedure until a condition becomes true. The form of these commands is

```
       until "a condition becomes true"
       do
            unix and shell commands
       done
```

or

```
       while "a condition is true"
       do
            unix and shell commands
       done
```

A loop will run forever if you choose a condition that is always true or never true, depending on your choice of commands. If you use the **until** command, the program becomes

```
       until test "a" = "b"
       do menu
       done
```

"a" is never "b." This loop will run forever—or until you select option 6 to exit. The overall structure is better illustrated if you insert the individual commands that belong to the menu shell script.

```
       until test "a" = "b"
       do
       pr -l24 -w78  TEXT
       read CHOICE
       case "$CHOICE" in
            1) DIR ;;
            2) TYPE ;;
            3) COPY ;;
            4) ERASE ;;
            5) RENAME ;;
```

```
        6) exit ;;
esac
done
```

If there is a problem with this shell script, it's that there is no pause between events. The only time anything stops is when you are forced to enter a selection or a filename. Let's put a pause into the program between the **esac** and the **done**.

```
until test "a" = "b"
do
pr -l24 -w78  TEXT
read CHOICE
case "$CHOICE" in
        1) DIR ;;
        2) TYPE ;;
        3) COPY ;;
        4) ERASE ;;
        5) RENAME ;;
        6) exit ;;
esac
echo "Press the RETURN key to continue..."
read PAUSE
done
```

Use the **chmod** command to make all of your shell scripts into commands.

ERASING THE SCREEN

You can write a shell script to clear (erase) your terminal screen. To do so, you will need to use the manual for your terminal. On most terminals, the screen is erased by sending an Escape followed by a specific character. Your manual will tell you which character to use. On ANSI standard terminals, such as those that come with the AT&T 3B2 and 3B5, use Escape followed by [and H and another Escape followed by [and J

to clear the screen. Create a program to clear the screen for ANSI standard terminals with

```
$ cat > clear
echo "<Esc>[H<Esc>[J"
^D
$ chmod u=rx clear
```

Use the **cat** command to enter the commands. The only shell command needed in this case is **echo**. Enter a double quote and press the Escape key. Escape is not a printable character. You won't see anything happen. Next, press [and **H** and then press the Escape key again and then [and **J** (or the clear screen characters from your manual). When you enter this, your screen may clear and the cursor may be positioned to the top left corner of your terminal screen. Now enter the closing double quote (''), press Return, and press **^D** to save your program. This will take you back to the shell prompt ($). Use the **chmod** command to make **clear** an executable program. From now on, any time that you want to clear the screen, type **clear** after a shell prompt.

POSITIONING THE CURSOR

Use the **echo** command to position the cursor to a specific location on the screen. In the menu program, the cursor ended up at the bottom left corner of the screen. Let's place the cursor on the line beginning with "Enter . . .", as shown in the modified menu screen below:

```
1  -    Display the disk directory
2  -    Display contents of a file
3  -    Copy a file
4  -    Erase a file
5  -    Rename a file
6  -    Exit back to UNIX
□       Enter the Number for Your Selection
        Then press the Return Key
```

We can accomplish this trick with the help of the **echo** command and the Escape key. Nearly all modern terminals allow you to specify where the cursor is to be located. This is called addressing the cursor. We can use this feature to write to any desired place on the screen.

Your terminal manual will explain how the cursor is addressed. The exact charactistics vary from terminal to terminal. ANSI standard terminals (such as the AT&T 3B2 and 3B5) use the format

<Esc>[row; column H

to position the cursor to a particular screen location. To demonstrate, let's write a command to print "This is 16,40" on row 16, beginning with column 40.

```
$ cat > demo
echo "<Esc>[16;40HThis is 16,40"
^D
```

Remember, <Esc> is our representation for the Escape key. When you are entering this sequence, you will not see the Escape. It is a nonprintable character. In addition, the cursor may jump around on the screen while you are entering the sequence. On many terminals, the cursor will be positioned to row 16, column 40, when you begin to enter the "T" of "This." Once the line is printed, the cursor will return to the beginning of the following line. To keep the cursor from advancing to the beginning of the following line, end the **echo** command with **\c** as shown below.

```
$ cat > demo
echo "<Esc>[16;40HThis is 16,40\c"
^D
```

The Televideo 950 uses "Escape = row column." The row and column values are often entered (as is the case with the Televideo 950) using printable ASCII characters (see Appendix 3). The first line on the screen is line number 1 (on some terminals it is

called line number 0). With the Televideo this is represented by a blank space. To position the cursor on row 16, column 40, use (on the Televideo 950)

```
$ cat > demo
echo "<Esc>=/FThis is 16,40\c"
^D
```

/ is the 16th printable ASCII character and F is the 40th printable ASCII character.

To illustrate the use of this technique, lets put all of this together modifying our menu program. The modified program is shown below. This incorporates the TEXT directly into the menu program. It has the added advantage of clearing the screen each time the menu is displayed as well as clearing the screen between the menu and the command response. This means you don't need to worry about the number of lines in the menu (provided that you don't exceed the screen's capability). The execution of the menu is also much crisper. Incidentally, you should notice the backslash (\) in front of the dollar sign ($) on the line for option 1. The dollar sign is interpreted by the shell as a special character. The backslash causes the shell to properly interpret the dollar sign.

For ANSI standard terminals use

```
$ cat > menu
until test "a" = "b"
do
echo "<Esc>[H<Esc>[J"
echo "<Esc>[5;20H1  - Display the disk Directory"
echo "<Esc>[7;20H2  - Display contents of a file"
echo "<Esc>[9;20H3  - Copy a file"
echo "<Esc>[11;20H3 - Erase a file"
echo "<Esc>[13;20H5 - Rename a file"
echo "<Esc>[15;20H6 - Exit back to UNIX"
echo "<Esc>[17;24HEnter the Number for Your Selection"
echo "<Esc>[18;24HThen press the Return Key"
echo "<Esc>[17;20H\c"
        read CHOICE
        echo "<Esc>[H<Esc>[J"
        case "$CHOICE" in
```

```
             1) DIR ;;
             2) TYPE ;;
             3) COPY ;;
             4) ERASE ;;
             5) RENAME ;;
             6) exit ;;
      esac
      echo "Press the RETURN key to continue...\c"
             read PAUSE
      done
      ^D
```

Create the command using **cat**. To edit the file, you can use the **vi** editor. When you edit it, the invisible (nonprintable) characters will become visible. The Escape will be displayed as "^[". All control characters have a leading ^ to indicate them.

SPECIAL DISPLAYS

You may sometimes want the program to control itself. For example, suppose you want a directory display where the ordinary disk files are displayed in alphabetical order and the subdirectory names are displayed in alphabetical order with the symbol <D> in front of their names. And, you want the filenames displayed in four columns. The table below shows the display you want.

aardvarks	inventory	Memotoed	<D> Clients
dBASE	insurance	Miscfiles	<D> Stocks
Framework	letter1	newdata	
Friday	letter2	<D> accounts	

By creating two commands you can make such a display. The first examines each filename in the directory and adds either blank spaces or a <D> to the displayed filename. This can be accomplished with the **for** command. This command has the format

```
for variable in list
do
      shell commands
done
```

and when you translate this sequence into actual commands it becomes

```
for FILE in *
do
      if test -d $FILE
          then echo "<D> $FILE"
          else echo "    $FILE"
      fi
done
```

In this program, the command **for** examines each filename in the directory and, one by one, places the filename in the variable "FILE." There is nothing significant about the name of the variable other than it makes the program easy to read. The variable could be named "GZYIWHIC" and the program would still perform in exactly the same way. We have indicated the entire directory as the list by using the star. We can restrict the amount of the directory by adding to the asterisk. For example, using **Ma*** would process only the filenames beginning with **Ma**.

Let's call this program "SHOW-1." The output of "SHOW-1" is a list (in the alphabetical order of the filenames) with either four blank spaces or <D> and one blank space displayed in front of the filename. To make "SHOW-1" into a program, use the **chmod** command.

```
$ chmod u=rwx SHOW-1
```

Next, create a command called **SHOW**. This command will use "SHOW-1" as a part of a pipeline.

```
$ cat > SHOW
clear
```

```
SHOW-1 | sort | pr -4 -l23 -w78 -h "Special Directory"
echo "press any key to continue...\c"
read PAUSE
^D
```

MAKING YOUR OWN COMMAND SET

At this point, your custom directory command is only available from the directory you were using when you created **DIR**. You can instruct UNIX to look for this command in a special directory called "PCDOS." To do this, create a directory named "PCDOS." We are using uppercase letters for all of our PCDOS conversion names just so they will stand out from standard UNIX commands.

```
$ mkdir PCDOS
```

When you tell UNIX to use a command such as **ls** or **mkdir**, it searches specific directories for those commands. It knows which directories to search by means of a variable named ".profile." You can look at this file with the **cat** command. A sample ".profile" file is shown. The ".profile" on your computer may vary substantially.

```
$cat .profile
umask 7
stty erase ^H kill ^U echoe intr ^C
TERM=tvi950
export TERM
TZ=PST8PDT
export TZ
PATH=:/usr/local/bin:/usr/bin:/bin
export PATH
```

The item of interest here is the line beginning with PATH. This defines the directories that are searched automatically and the order in which they are searched. Notice that they use the absolute pathnames for the directories and that the colon is used at the

beginning of each pathname. To insert our new command directory into the automatic search path, use any of the standard editors **ed** or **vi** (or a word processor).

First get the absolute pathname for your PCDOS directory. This procedure and display should looks like the following:

```
$ cd PCDOS          select directory PCDOS
$ pwd               print working directory
/02/byers/PCDOS     absolute pathname
$ cd ..             return to original
```

Note that I have assumed you were in your home directory, the directory that you are in when you first enter UNIX. Next, using one of the editing tools, insert a colon and the absolute pathname of your PCDOS directory at the end of the PATH line. Our sample PATH becomes

```
PATH=:/usr/local/bin:/usr/bin:/bin:/02/byers/PCDOS
```

You can change the prompt to "C>" while you are editing ".profile." To do this, add the two lines

```
PS1='C>'
export PS1
```

to the end of the file. Shell variables, such as PS1, are discarded when you exit from a shell script. The command **export** causes the shell to remember the variable and its contents even after you have left the shell script.

Now, move your commands **DIR** and **dir** into the directory PCDOS:

```
$ mv DIR PCDOS
$ mv dir PCDOS
```

To have UNIX read your changes, you must exit from UNIX and log back in. The ".profile" file is read during the login process. When you re-enter, the prompt will be a C> instead of a $ and you will be able to access your directory command from *any* of

your directories with only its simple filename. By the way, if you have done anything wrong, you may have some small difficulty when you re-enter. If it's something you can't deal with yourself, see your system administrator.

In this chapter, you have learned how to write shell scripts. Creating a set of custom commands, as we did, illustrates the power and flexibility of the UNIX system and how you can adapt its capabilities and resources to your own needs.

APPENDIX 1

ed, vi, and nroff

In this appendix, the text editors **ed** and **vi** and the text formatter **nroff** (introduced in Chapter 7) are discussed in greater detail. The **ed** line editor section covers the editing of existing files, searching files, copying text, editing commands, and undoing mistakes. The **vi** section covers editing with this screen editor and includes a table of **vi** commands. The section on the **nroff** text formatter also has a table of commands and uses examples to explain using the **nroff** commands to print out headers, titles, subscripts, superscripts, and page numbers; and to format lines and paragraphs, to set up macros to save format lines and paragraphs, to set up macros to save keystrokes when inserting commands, and to format columns and tables.

Using ed to Edit an Existing Text File

If we were all perfect typists and never changed our minds, we wouldn't need word processors or text editors. Typewriters are much cheaper and easier to use. The value of word processors and text editors lies in their editing capabilities.

The **ed** text editor was introduced in Chapter 7. The table below shows the **ed** commands:

BASIC COMMAND SUMMARY FOR THE **ed** LINE EDITOR

< >   indicates item is optional
N   is the starting line number
X   is the ending line number
R   is the Range and can be either g (global) or N, X . .

Q	Abort
<N>a	Add new lines of text after current line
<N>c	Change (overwrite) existing text
<N>r <filename>	Copy from another file to line N
<N,X>d	Delete line(s) of text
<N><,><X>n	Display text with line numbers
<N><,><X>p	Display text without line numbers
.=	Display current line number
q	Exit
<N>i	Insert new lines before current line
N	Position to line number N
<N,X>mY	Move text to line Y
P	Prompt on/off
w	Save
<R>/pattern/<n>	Search and display lines containing pattern
<R>s/P1/P2/<g>	Search and replace Pattern P1 with Pattern P2
u	Undo the last command
<N,X>w <filename>	Write to another file

SPECIAL CHARACTERS IN ed

.	Use at beginning of line to exit from entry mode (used with commands a,i, and c)
.	Substitute for single character in search pattern
.	Current line
,	Use in front of n or p (i.e. ,p) for entire file
$	Last Line
$	Search pattern must end the line
^	Search Pattern must begin the line
\	Character following \ is not "special"

*	Substitute for group of characters in search pattern
/	Search Forward
?	Search Backward
g	Global

To edit (change) an existing file, type **ed** and the filename at the UNIX prompt. The command is exactly the same as when you create a file (see Chapter 7). For example, to edit the file "memo," type **ed memo** and the computer responds with

```
$ ed memo
44
□
```

ed responded to the command **ed memo** by displaying the number of characters (bytes) that are in the file. When you created the file, the response was the error signal (the "?") followed by the filename. The two responses provide you with some protection against attempting to edit an existing file but inadvertently misspelling the filename.

When you edit a file, you are actually editing a copy of the file and not the file itself. This feature makes it possible for you to change your mind and abandon your changes without affecting the original file. The copy is automatically created when you invoke the editor. This copy resides in a special temporary file called a "buffer." This temporary file can be as large as 128,000 bytes. The average printed page has about 2,000 characters. This buffer holds about 64 standard pages of text. The **w** (write) command will overwrite your original file with the edited version in the buffer.

At this point, you are in **ed**'s command mode. To have the command mode prompt displayed, type **P** and a Return. The display

```
$ ed memo
44
P
*□
```

tells you that you are ready to begin editing. You edit one line at a time. You must tell **ed** which line you want to edit. Each line of text in the file has a line number. The first line is number 1. The line you are editing, the current line, can be represented by either a period—called the "dot"—or by its line number. The last line in the file can be referred to by either the dollar sign "$", or its line number.

Let's demonstrate file editing by adding a new line, "I am fine." to the "memo" file after the "How are you?" line. Add the line by first entering the line number of "How are you?" and a Return. This positions the file to line number two and then displays line two. Line number two is now the current line. Next, use the append command **a** to get into input mode. Then, enter your new line. Use the dot (.) to exit from the input mode. Save your changes by using the **w** (write) command.

`*2`	go to line 2
`How are you?`	current line
`*a`	append after current line
`I am fine.`	enter text
`.`	exit from input mode
`*w`	save the changes
`60`	size of file (characters)
`*□`	

Viewing the File You can look at either selected lines or the entire file by using the **p** (print) command. Again, most references to printing in UNIX really mean "display." When UNIX was originally developed, the user and the computer communicated through printing terminals. Today, of course, we use video terminals. Hardcopy is printed separately using one of the printers attached to the computer. Use a comma in front of the print command, as in the example,

```
*,p
Dear Reader:
     How are you?
     I am fine.
Your Author.
*□
```

to view the entire file. To view the file and display the line numbers, use the **n** command. Both **n** and **p** display the contents of the file.

```
*,n
1     Dear Reader:
2          How are you?
3          I am fine.
4     Your Author.
*□
```

You can view just a selected section of the file. For example, let's suppose you want to view lines 2 and 3. The command (and the response) will be

```
*2,3p                              display lines 2 thru 3
     How are you?
     I am fine.
*□
```

Many of the editor commands allow you to specify a range of command lines to which the command applies. In general, a command consists of an optional address and the command. If the optional address is omitted, the command is understood to apply to the current line.

The editor keeps track of where you are in the file. The current line is line 3 ("I am fine."). Using the dot with an equals sign

```
* .=                                    Where am I?
3                                        On this line
*□
```

will get you your current line number. Using the equal sign alone

```
*=                                       How many lines?
4                                        This many
*□
```

will show how many lines there are in the file. Using the commands **.,$p** or **;p**

```
*;p
          I am fine.
Your Author.
*□
```

you can display from where you are to the end of the file.

Our sample file has only four lines at present, so determining the line number isn't difficult. Determining the line number isn't quite so straightforward once you have a large document and you are adding and deleting lines. Fortunately, you can also use **ed** to locate a particular line based on the content of the line.

Searching Files You can have the editor search the file for a particular sequence of characters (a character string) by enclosing the character string in slashes (/). For example, let's search the file for the character string "How ar":

```
*1                                       go to the beginning
Dear Reader:                             ok
*/How ar/                                search for How ar
        How are you?                     Found it
* .=                                     Where am I?
2                                        You're on this line
*□
```

The string must consist of a contiguous set of characters. The search begins with the current line and ends when a match is found.

The editor tells you that it has found the character string by displaying the line containing the specified character string. It's important to note that the character string does not have to begin the line. In fact, in this example, "How ar" does *not* begin the second line. The second line actually begins with five blank spaces. You can combine the search command with another command such as **n**

```
*1                        go to the beginning
Dear Reader:              ok
*/How ar/n                search for "How ar"
2     How are you?        Found it as line 2
*□
```

with the slashes (/) indicating that you want to search in the forward direction, that is, toward the end of the file. You can also search in the reverse direction, that is, toward the beginning of the file, by enclosing the character string in question marks. To illustrate, let's search from the end of the file for the string "How ar":

```
*$                        go to the end of the file.
Your Author.              ok
*?How ar?n                search for "How ar"
2     How are you?        Found it as line 2
*□
```

In either case, you must enclose enough of the line to identify it uniquely. The search will end with the first hit. If there were two lines in our document that contained the word "How" the search would stop at the first of those two lines.

You can also display all of the lines that contain a particular character string. For example, you can display all lines that contain a lowercase " a" by simply preceding the search pattern with a **g** (global):

```
*$                                        go to the end
Your Author.
*g/a/                                     global search

Dear Reader:                             found it
How are you?                             found another
I am fine.                               and another
*□
```

Note that, even though the search began when you were positioned to the last record, the global search began with line 1. Line 4 was not displayed because it does not contain a lowercase "a." You will get exactly the same result whether you use the slashes or the question marks in a global search.

It is advisable to always add the **n** command when doing a global search, so that the line number is displayed along with the line.

```
*g/a/n
1      Dear Reader:                      found it
2            How are you?                found another
3            I am fine.                  and another
*□
```

You can also display all of the lines that do not contain the desired search pattern. In the example above, all of the lines that contained a lowercase "a" were displayed. To display all of the that do *not* contain a lowercase "a," use the **v** instead of the **g**, as shown below:

```
*v/a/n
4      Your Author.
*□
```

There are a number of special characters that you can use to help you in your search. These are the ^ (caret), $ (dollar sign), dot (.), and the asterisk (*). These characters are sometimes called the *metacharacters.* They can occur in the text. If they are

a part of your search pattern, they must be set off by the \ (backslash). For example, to search for the pattern "Author.", you need to indicate that the period is part of the search pattern (otherwise it is a wildcard):

```
*/Author\./
Your Author.
*□
```

The caret is used to indicate that the search pattern *must* occur at the beginning of the line. Let's use the caret with our search for "How ar":

```
*1                        go to the beginning
Dear Reader:              ok
*/^How ar/                search
?                         didn't find it
*□
```

and the result is the question mark, which is an error message. In this case, the question mark tells us that our search is unsuccessful, because the line in question actually begins with 5 blank spaces. Use

```
*1
Dear Reader
*/^     How ar/
2
*□
```

to search for this line.

The "$" indicates the last line in the file. It can also be used to indicate the last item on a line. If you search for a line ending with "Author"

```
*1
Dear Reader
*/Author$/
?
*□
```

the search is unsuccessful because the period was not included. The last item on the line means the last item on the line. Use

```
*1
Dear Reader
*/Author\ $/
?
*□
```

to conduct a successful search. Note that you had to use the backslash before the period—because the dot is a metacharacter. The slash indicates that the dot in this search pattern actually is a period.

The dot can be used in a search pattern as a wildcard to represent any character. It is useful when you don't know the exact spelling of a word or name, and for displaying items with common elements. For example,

```
*g/f.ll/
```

will display all lines that contain such words as befall, fill, fall, full, fuller, and so on. The command

```
*g/.ou./n
2          How are you?              .ou. = you?
4      Your Author.                  .ou. = Your
*□
```

will locate the sequence "ou" in our sample file memo.

```
*g/ou.*/n
2            How are you?              ou.* = you?
4       Your Author.                   ou.* = Your
*□
```

The dot (.) followed by the star (*) is used to indicate the remainder of a word. In this case the star signifies zero or more single character wildcards (the dot). Be careful when you use the star as part of a search pattern. It has the same characteristics within **ed** and **vi** as it does in **grep**.

```
*g/X*/
Dear Reader:
     How are you?
     I am fine.
Your Author.
*□
```

Search and Replace You can search for a pattern (sequence) in your document and then replace that pattern with another that you have specified. For example, you can substitute "you today" for the existing pattern "you" in our example file "memo." The command to "find and replace" is **s** (substitute). In the following example, position to line 2:

```
*2                              go to line 2
How are you?                    ok
*s/you/you today/               substitute
*p                              display current line
*□
```

and then, substitute "you today" for the single occurrence of "you." If there had been multiple occurrences of the pattern "you" on this line, the substitution would only apply to the first occurrence. Add a **g** to the end of the command

```
*s/you/you today/g
```

to make the substitution for all occurrences. The command

        *2,4s/you/you today/g

will search the second through the fourth lines and make the substitution everywhere that it is applicable on these lines. You must specify both the beginning line and the ending line. Using

        *g/you/s//you today/g   global substitution

will make the substitutions global; that is, the changes will be made throughout the file.

   Copying Text You can copy selected text from this file (the one you are editing) to a new file. This is accomplished by a variation of the **w** (write) command. With the command

        *2,3w memo1

you can copy lines 2 through 3 to a new file named "memo1". The command

        *w memo1

will copy all of our example file to the new file "memo1".

   Copying Text from Another File You can copy the contents of another file into the file being edited. The copy operation is accomplished by the **r** (read) command. The file being copied will be added just after the current line. To illustrate, the file "letter" contains the lines:

        The weather has been good.
        I hope to be home soon.

To copy the contents of "letter" into the example file, the command (using **r**)

ed, vi, and nroff

```
*3r letter
*,n
1      Dear Reader:
2           How are you today?
3           I am fine.
4           The weather has been good.
5           I hope to be home soon.
6      Your Author.
*
```

will place the new text just after line 3.

Editing Lines of Text Use the **m** command to move one or more lines from one position in the file to another. The lines to be moved with a single use of the command *must* be consecutive. For example,

```
*3,5m6
*,n
1      Dear Reader:
2           How are you today?
3      Your Author.
4           I am fine.
5           The weather has been good.
6           I hope to be home soon.
*□
```

will move lines 3 through 5 from their current position to the end of the file (after line 6). Use

```
*4m2
*,n
1     Dear Reader:
2         How are you today?
3         I am fine.
4     Your Author.
5         The weather has been good.
6         I hope to be home soon.
*□
```

to move line 4 back to just after line 2.

Deleting Lines Remove unwanted lines with the **d** (delete) command. This command will remove one or more consecutive lines of text. For example,

```
*5,6d
*,n
1     Dear Reader:
2         How are you today?
3         I am fine.
4     Your Author.
*□
```

will remove lines 5 and 6 from our example file.

Adding Lines Add new lines of text by using the **a** (append) command just as when created the file originally. The new text will be added after the current line. Add new lines to the file between the current lines 1 and 2 with the command

```
*1a                          insert before line 1
I wish you were here         new text
.                            exit from insert
*□
```

which specifies a line number just before the append command. You can also use the **i** (insert) command to insert lines. The new lines are inserted just before the current line. The following example

```
*2i                               insert before line 2
I  wish  you  were  here          new text
.                                 exit from insert
*□
```

produces exactly the same result as the append example above. The result

```
*,n
1     Dear Reader:
2     I  wish  you  were  here
3          How  are  you  today?
4          I  am  fine.
5     Your  Author.
*□
```

will be produced from either of these last two examples.

Changing Lines of Text The **c** (change) command allows you to replace existing lines with new lines. You can change one or more lines with **c**. When more than one line is changed, the lines must be consecutive. The change command requires that you retype each of the specified lines. To change (edit) a single word, use the substitute command. To illustrate the change command, retype line 2, adding 5 blank spaces to the beginning:

```
*2c                                    retype line 2
      I  really  wish  you  were  here.   ok
.                                      done
*,n
1     Dear  Reader:
2          I  really  wish  you  were  here.
```

```
3          How are you today?
4            I am fine.
5      Your Author.
*□
```

Notice that the dot (.) is still needed to tell the editor the changes are finished. If you had gone ahead and typed three more lines, the change command would have substituted the first line for the existing line two and added the three new lines before the current line 3. Similarly, had you specified that you wanted to change lines 2 through 4 (2,4c) and retyped only line 2 as above, the current lines 3 and 4 would be deleted. The change command allows you to retype lines, retype and append, retype and delete.

Undoing Mistakes The last command that changed anything in your file can be undone with the **u** (undo) command. This command takes you back one change. Note that you can have any number of display or search commands between the change to be undone and the use of **u**. The command

```
*u                                   undo the last change
*,n
1      Dear Reader:
2      I wish you were here
3          How are you today?
4            I am fine.
5      Your Author.
*□
```

will undo our last change.

As you type each line, sooner or later you will make a typing error. To correct the error, use the backspace key to erase the character and type the correct character in its place. The erase character may vary from terminal to terminal. On some terminals it may be labeled "backspace," on others "rub," and on still others it may simply be an arrow pointing backwards.

Your UNIX manual may tell you to use the "#" (pound sign) to cancel the last character. Try it—and hope it doesn't work. The "#" was used to cancel the last

character on teletypes in the 1960s and early 1970s. It's about time AT&T accepted the fact that most of us use video terminals on our computers.

Editing a File with vi

vi is a part of the Berkeley version of UNIX; it was developed by William Joy of the University of California at Berkeley. Chapter 7 introduced you to this screen editor and showed you how to create a file. This section will cover moving the cursor, editing a file, searching for text, duplicating text, and other features.

To edit an existing file with **vi**, type **vi** followed by the name of the file. For example, type

```
$ vi demo
```

to edit the file "demo." The contents of the file "demo"

```
Dear Reader:
This is the vi editor.
Your Author.
+
~
~
~

"demo" 4 lines, 55 characters
```

is displayed beginning at the upper left-hand corner of the window. If the file has more lines than can be displayed by the window, one windowful (screenful) will be displayed. The filename, the number of lines, and the total number of characters in the file are displayed at the bottom of the screen. The cursor is positioned at the beginning of the window.

Fixing Typing Errors You will most often use the text editor first to fix typos. Suppose you had actually entered the second line as

```
Ths is tje vi editoor.
```

This sample line has everything: a missing letter, an erroneous letter, and one letter two many.

Moving the Cursor The first step in repairing your file is to move the cursor to the position of the error. The cursor is moved in the command mode. If your terminal has arrow keys (most do), you should be able to use these keys to move around in the file. If not, use the keys "h," "j," "k," and "l."

arrow key	letter key	direction
up	k	up one line
down	j	down one line
left	h	left one character
right	l	right one character

Adding a Character There are two ways to add a letter: append and insert. The *append* command adds characters to the right of the cursor position. The *insert* command adds characters to the left of the cursor position. Both commands allow you to add characters until you terminate the process with Escape. Use one of the following procedures to add the letter "i" to the word "ths":

APPENDING

move the cursor to the "h"
press the **a** (append) key
enter the letter "i"
press the Escape key

INSERTING

> move the cursor to the "s"
> press the **i** (insert) key
> enter the letter "i"
> press the Escape key

As you can see, both procedures are straightforward and there is little difference between appending and inserting. Both examples convert "ths" to "this". Our poorly typed line now reads:

> This is tje vi editoor.

Changing a Letter To replace one letter with another, use the **r** (replace) command. Let's replace the erroneous "j" with the proper "h" in the word "tje". This procedure

> move the cursor to the "j" in "tje"
> press the **r** (replace) key
> enter the letter "h"

will show how to replace "tje" with "the" in our example line; it now reads:

> This is the vi editoor.

Deleting a Character "Editoor" is a creative way of spelling editor. To remove the extra "o," you use the **x** command. This command is sometimes called the "gobble" command and it is used in this way:

> move the cursor to an "o" in "editoor"
> press the **x** (gobble) key

Note that you do *not* need to enter the Escape. It will not hurt anything if you do, but it isn't needed. "Editor" is now spelled correctly, and the line is now:

This is the vi editor.

Be sure to use the lowercase **x**. Use of the uppercase **X** will delete the character to the left of the cursor.

Inserting a Word Let's insert the word "Berkeley" into our sample sentence so that it reads "This is the Berkeley vi editor." Adding a word is accomplished in the same way as adding a single letter. Use either the append or insert commands.

APPENDING

> move the cursor to the space before "vi"
> press the **a** (append) key
> type in the word "Berkeley"
> press the space bar
> press the Escape key

INSERTING

> move the cursor to the "v" of "vi"
> press the **i** (insert) key
> enter the word "Berkeley"
> press the space bar
> press the Escape key

You must remember to add the blank space after the word.

Deleting a Word Now, fickle as ever, you wish to remove the word "Berkeley" from the sentence. You have an option. You can use either the **x** (gobble) command or the **dw** (delete word) command. The easy way

> place the cursor on the "B" of "Berkeley"
> press the **x** key until the word disappears

uses the **x** command. The easier way

> place the cursor on the "B" of "Berkeley"
> press the **d** key
> press the **w** key

uses the **dw** command.

If you use the gobble command, remember that the uppercase **X** removes characters to the left of the cursor. If the cursor is not placed at the beginning of the word, the part of the word from the cursor to the next space is removed. If you delete a whole word, the space after that word is also removed so that the proper word spacing is preserved.

Inserting a Line You can use either the **i** (insert) or the **a** (append) command to add a new line anywhere in your document. Using **i** (insert)

> place the cursor at the beginning of the line
> press the **i** (insert) key
> press the Return key
> enter text if desired
> press Escape

adds a line before the current line. Using **a** (append)

> place the cursor at the end of the line
> press the **a** (append) key
> press the Return key
> enter text if desired
> press Escape

adds a line after the current line. Adding "vi is an example of a screen editor" as a new line just before "Your Author" with this procedure

      place the cursor on the "Y" of "Your"
      press the **i** key
      press the <return key>
      type in "vi is an example of a screen editor"
      press Escape

will illustrate the use of these commands.

      Deleting All or Part of a Line You can delete: all of a line; from the beginning of the line to the cursor; from the cursor to the end of the line.

The **dd** (delete line) command

      place the cursor on the line to be deleted
      press the **d** key twice (**dd**)

deletes a whole line. Use the **d^** command

      place the cursor on the line
      place the cursor on the last character to be deleted
      press the **d** key
      press the ^ key

to delete the first part of a line. The **$** command

      place the cursor on the line
      place the cursor on the first character to be deleted
      press the **d** key
      press the **$** key

will delete the the last part of a line.
      Note that in all three cases the character to which the cursor is positioned is deleted. On some systems, the deleted line may appear as a blank line. When this

happens press the Control key and the "r" key together **^r.** This step will cause the **vi** editor to redraw the display window.

Duplicating Text It is often convenient to duplicate a part of the document you are editing. You can type the information in twice or you can use the tools provided by **vi** for copying text. These tools are called **yank** and **put**. **yank** is used to identify the text to be duplicated. A copy of this text is placed in a temporary buffer. **put** copies this text from the buffer back into your file at the place you want it. Let's duplicate the second line of our sample file "demo":

```
Dear Reader:
        This is the vi editor.
Your Author.
```

Our first step is to identify the block of text that is to be copied. This is accomplished by moving the cursor to the beginning of the lines to be copied. The command consists of the number of lines to be copied followed by a capital "Y."

Then the copying operation is completed by using the **put** command. There are two forms of **put**: the lowercase **p** and the uppercase **P**. The lowercase **p** inserts the lines just *after* the current line. The uppercase **P** inserts the lines just *before* the current line. After you follow these steps

```
place the cursor at the beginning of line 2
press the 1 key
press the Y key
press the p key
```

the file reads:

```
Dear Reader:
        This is the vi editor.
        This is the vi editor.
Your Author.
```

You can make as many copies of this line as you like, by pressing either **p** or **P**. Each time you press either key, the block of text will be copied.

You can also make copies of one or more words by using the **yank**ing with the lowercase **yw**. The words are duplicated by moving the cursor to the desired location and pressing the lowercase **p**. Line 2 will end with the words "vi editor" repeated a total of three times after you use this command series

> place the cursor on the "v" of vi.
> press the **2** key (number of words)
> press the **y** key
> press the **w** key
> press the **p** key twice

and so, the file now reads:

```
Dear Reader:
        This is the vi editor vi editor vi editor.
        This is the vi editor.
Your Author.
```

The **yank** command identifies words or lines of text that are to be copied. **yw** identifies words. **Y** identifies lines. The preceeding number represents the number of words or lines in the block. The words or lines begin with the current cursor position. The **put** command is used to duplicate the text identified by **yank**. Do not make any changes or deletions to your document between the **yank** and **put** commands because the words or lines that are deleted, changed, or yanked are all copied to the same buffer.

Moving Blocks of Text You can move words or lines from one location in your document to another—by combining the **delete** and **put** commands. When you delete something, the words or lines are first copied to a buffer—in case you change your mind. The **put** command reads that buffer and, as you have seen, copies it back into your file at the current position of the cursor.

To demonstrate moving blocks of text, let's move lines 2 and 3 of our file "demo" to just after the signature "Your Author." The command sequence

place the cursor on line 2
press the **2** key   number of lines
press the **d** key twice   delete line
place the cursor on the "Y" of "Yours"
press the **p** key

will accomplish the move. The lines are now transferred so that the file now reads:

```
Dear Reader:
Your Author.
     This is the vi editor vi editor vi editor.
     This is the vi editor.
```

Undoing Changes You may change your mind somewhere during the editing process. You can undo the last change by using the lowercase **u** (undo). You can undo all changes to the current line and restore your file to the condition at the last **w** (write) command by using the uppercase **U**. In this example, you

Press the capital **U**

to restore the file its original condition, and the file becomes:

```
Dear Reader:
     This is the vi editor.
Your Author.
```

(restored to its form before the copying process).

Scrolling Through a Large File The file used in the above examples was small. You will usually be working with documents (files) that take much more than a single 24-line screen. You can scroll through a larger document with the help of the Control key. Remember, when using the Control key, to hold it down while striking the desired letter key.

Scrolling forward means scrolling toward the end of the file. Scrolling backward means scrolling toward the beginning of the file. Scrolling a half window means that

half of the previous window is retained. Scrolling a full window means that only two lines of the previous window remain for continuity. The scrolling commands are as follows:

Control - D	forward a half window
Control - F	forward a full window
Control - U	backward a half window
Control - B	backward a full window

Searching Files If the file is large, you may want to have the editor locate a particular word or phrase and redraw the screen with the cursor positioned to the beginning of the search key. This is done with the help of the slash (/), the search command. To search for the word "vi" in our sample file, you would

press the / key
type in the word "vi" (the search key)
press either Escape or Return

and the search will progress from the current cursor position to the end of the file. If the search key is not found, the search wraps around and searches from the beginning of the file to the position of the cursor. If the search pattern isn't found, the message "pattern not found" will be displayed at the bottom of the screen. If the pattern is found, the window readjusts so that the part of the file containing the search pattern is on screen. The cursor will be positioned to the beginning of the search pattern.

If there are multiple occurrences of the pattern, the search will stop at the first successful pattern match. If this isn't the desired occurrence, you can continue the search with **n**, the continue search command. To search the file in the backwards direction, use the **?** command, not the **/** command.

This appendix is intended to give you a working knowledge of the **vi** editor and to show you how to use its basic features. These features, as well as some other commands that were not discussed, are summarized in the following command table.

TABLE OF <u>vi</u> COMMANDS

< > indicates item is optional
N is a number
L is a letter

CURSOR CONTROLS

← or h	1 character left
→ or l	1 character right
↑ or k	1 line up
↓ or j	1 line down
^	beginning of line
$	end of line
H	beginning of window
M	middle of window
L	bottom of window
w	1 word right
e	move to end of word
b	move to beginning of word
fP	move to character P

SCROLLING COMMANDS

z	move current line to top of window
z.	move current line to center screen
z-	move current line to bottom of screen
^D	scroll down 1/2 window toward end of file
^U	scroll up 1/2 window toward beginning
^F	scroll full window toward end of file
^B	scroll full window foward beginning
NG or :N	scroll to line number N
G or :$	scroll to end of file
/Pattern	scroll to line matching pattern

APPENDIX 1

CHARACTERS WITH A SPECIAL MEANING IN **vi**

<ESC>	Use at beginning of line to exit from entry mode
$	Last Line
$	End of Line
^	Beginning of Line

MOVING TEXT

<L><N>yy	moves N lines of text beginning with the current line to the buffer <L>
<L>p	moves text from the buffer <L> to the current cursor position

EDITING COMMANDS

:q!	Abort
a	Add text after current cursor position
A	Add text at the end of the line
r	Change (overwrite) 1 character
R	Change (overwrite) several characters
C	Change to end of line
<N>cw	Change word(s)
<N>dd	Delete line(s) of text
d$	Delete to end of line
d^	Delete to beginning of line
d/pattern	Deletes pattern
<N>dw	Delete word(s) to right
<N>db	Delete word(s) to left
x	Delete character under the cursor
X	Delete character to left of cursor
:q	Exit
i	Insert text at current cursor position
I	Insert text at beginning of the line

NG	Position to line number N
^R	Redraw the screen
:w	Save
:wq	Save and exit
u	Undo the last command
U	Undo all changes made to this line

nroff Text Formatter

With the **nroff** text formatter, you can produce polished professional documents with commands inserted into your text using the **ed** or **vi** editors. Chapter 7 introduced the use of embedded formatting commands to layout a page of text for printing (or screen display). Figures 7-1, 7-2, and 7-3 traced the formatting of a sample business letter from straight text, to text plus **nroff** commands, to the printed output. Consult this formatting sample as you read the rest of this appendix.

The **nroff** formatting commands are summarized in the following table:

SUMMARY OF MAJOR **nroff** COMMANDS

.br	Break (next line starts a formatted line)
.ce N	Center Next N Lines
.de AB	Define Macro named AB
.wh N AB	Execute Macro Named AB when line is N
.fi	Filling On
.nf	Filling Off
.hn	Hyphenation Off
.hy	Hyphenxion On
.ti N	Indents 1 line N spaces from left margin
.in N	Indents Lines N spaces from left margin

APPENDIX 1

.in N	Indents Lines N spaces from left margin
.ll N	Line Length (in character spaces)
.ls N	Line Spacing in Lines
.po N	Margin, left (in character spaces)
	Margin, right = left margin + line length
	Margin, Top—use macro
	Margin, Bottom—use macro
.bp	Page Break (New Page)
.pl N	Page Length (paper size in lines)
.sp N	Print N Blank Lines
	Print Page Number (use a Macro)
.ad n	Right Justification Off
.na	Right Justification On
.pn N	Startin Page Number
\d	Subscript (half line down)
\u	Superscript (half line up)
.ta A,B,C	Tabs set at A, B, and C. Use for tables.
.tl 'L'C'R'	Title Line— L is left justified
	C is centered
	R is right justified
.lt N	Title line width
.ul N	Underline Next N unformatted lines
.cu N	Underline continuous Next N unformatted lines

Page Numbering The **nroff** formatter does not automatically print the page number, but it does keep track of the page number. To print the page number centered at the bottom of the page, you must modify the macro created for the bottom margin. A modified version of the macro MB is

```
.de MB                    define macro MB
.sp 2                     2 blank lines
.tl ''%''                 center & print page number
.bp                       begin new page
..                        end macro
```

and it includes the **sp 2** command to add two blank lines and the **tl** (title) command to center and print the page number. Note that the page number is represented by the percent sign (%). The percent sign is enclosed by two sets of single quotes. It is important that all four quotes be identical (use the apostrophe for all four).

Page numbering will automatically begin with page 1. If you wish to begin with a number other than 1, use the **pn** (page number) command. This command is useful for numbering pages consecutively when your document is a part (not the beginning) of a larger document. For example, you would use

```
.pn 87
```

if you want to begin numbering with page 87.

Centering You can center a line on the page with the **ce** (center) command. This command will center the following line of text. If you want to center the next 4 consecutive lines, you can use

```
.ce 4
```

but do not pad the front of your text with blank spaces. For example,

```
.ce
center this line
```

will produce a different output than

```
.ce
        center this line
```

because those extra spaces become a part of the line to center.

Page Title and Standard Headers You can define a standard header to be printed at the top of each page in your document. A header can have up to three separate parts: left, right, and center. The command

```
.tl 'left 'center'right'
```

will print titles. The left text will be left adjusted, the right text will be right adjusted, and the center text will be centered on the line. This command, exactly as it appears above, will display:

left   center   right

Omit the text between the rightmost single quotes

```
.tl 'left'''
```

to display just the left part. Similarly, to display only the right part, omit the text between the leftmost single quotes:

```
.tl '''right'
```

and to have the center text only use

```
.tl ''center''
```

Be sure to use only identical single quotes (apostrophes). Modifying the macro for the top margin to

```
.de MT                       define macro MT
.sp 4                        start page with 4 blanks
.tl ''Chapter 6''            page title
.sp 2
..
```

will incorporate the standard title "Chapter 6" into a page header to be printed on each page. Keep in mind that the page header is placed in the macro MT so that it will be printed at the top of the page. Printing in that case is caused by the **wh** trap. You can also use the **tl** command anywhere within the text of your document. You can use the

command to print footnotes. If you do, you should include the **tl** lines within the macro for the bottom of the page.

You can also adjust the width of the title line so that it is wider than, narrower than, or the same width as the body of the text. The command

        `.lt 65`

sets the title line width to 65 characters. You do not need to use the **lt** command if the title width is to be 65 characters.

Blank Lines Blank lines are often used to set off paragraphs, titles, and key points. You can use the Return key while editing to insert blank lines into your text. These lines will appear as blanks when displaying or printing your document with almost any process except the "**roffs**". The formatters will join these lines to the preceding lines. Remember that what you see on the screen may not be what you get on paper.

The proper way of printing blank lines is with the **sp** (space) command. You can use this command to create one or more blanks. To create a single blank line, use

        `.sp`

without an argument. To create 5 blank lines, follow the command with the number of consecutive blank lines you wish.

        `.sp 5`

The **sp** command must be used at every location where a blank line is desired.

Line Spacing You can control the basic line spacing of your document with the **ls** (line space) command. Unless you specify otherwise, the document is set for single spacing automatically. For double spacing, use

        `.ls 2`

and use

        `.ls 3`

for triple spacing. If you have set the line spacing to other than single spacing, you must use

. ls 1

to return to single spacing.

Starting a New Page You have already used the **bp** (begin page) command to start a new page in the bottom margin macro MB. Use the **bp** command any time that you wish to start a new page. Perhaps you want a topic to begin at the top of a page. Unless you place a **bp** command just before the topic, it will only begin the page if, by chance, it occurs exactly where the page break falls.

If you want to format and print your document in two-column (magazine) format, you will need to use the **col** program. The **nroff** formatting command for two-column printing requires that your printer be capable of backing up (reverse line feeds). Backing up more than a half line is not a good idea on most printers. The **col** program accepts your multi-column formatted document and uses the computer's memory to build up each page for printing. You would send the file to the printer with the command

$ nroff letter | col | lp

if you had formatted the file "letter" for two-column output.

Macros With **nroff**, you can define your own formatting commands, called *macros*. Each macro must consist of one or more standard **nroff** commands. You'll remember the macros discussed in the section on setting top and bottom margins. Macros are most often used when the same set of commands is repeated several times within a document, such as for setting the top margin and the bottom margin, and for paragraph definition. Macros save you work and make your file easier to read.

Macros must begin with the **de** (define macro) command. This command tells **nroff** the macro name and that the following standard commands belong to the macro but are not to be executed now. The macro name can consist of one or two letters. It's a good idea to use capital letters for the macro name, so that you can distinguish it from the standard command names, which are all in lowercase.

Macros end with two dots (..). This signal tells **nroff** that you have finished with the definition of the macro. Although it's not necessary, it's a good idea to define all of your macros at the beginning of your document. If you do, then you know exactly where to look for the definition of a particular macro—which can be helpful when editing a large document.

The sample business letter in Figure 7-3 (see Chapter 7) illustrates the definition and use of macros. The edited letter, including the formatting commands, is shown as Figure 7-2. Note that this letter begins with the definition of three macros: the top margin, the bottom margin, and a simple paragraph control for standard indented paragraphs. These macros are reasonably standard for a good many documents, even in this example where the bottom margin is not really needed.

You can avoid entering standard macros, such as those shown in the example, by creating a file that contains only those macros. After you have entered your basic letter and are ready to begin entering the formatting commands, copy this macro file into your document. Files of standard macros are often available on most UNIX computers. For general purpose use, however, it is probably more bother to learn to use these so-called standard macros than it is to create your own macro library.

Line Formatting The next step is to understand how **nroff** handles lines of text. Once again, what you see when editing may *not* be what you get out of **nroff**: It will attempt to combine lines into longer lines so that the length of a line is approximately the same (but not longer than) as the line length specified by the **ll** command. Let's suppose that you entered the following text with the text editor and the line length is set to 41. Before **nroff**, the text will look like the following:

```
.ll 41
Mary had a little lamb.
Its fleece was white as snow.
Everywhere that Mary Went
The lamb was sure to go.
```

When formatted by **nroff**, the text looks like this:

```
Mary  had  a  little  lamb.   Its  fleece  was
white  as  snow.   Everywhere  that  Mary  Went
The  lamb  was  sure  to  go.
```

You can take advantage of this when creating and editing the document. Notice that **nroff** was smart enought to insert two blank spaces following a period. A sentence can overlap lines and be accurately assembled into a paragraph.

This poem has been assembled into a paragraph with a ragged right margin. It looks as if it has been typed on a typewriter. **nroff** will format these lines into a paragraph with a justified right margin, unless you specify otherwise. This is done by *filling* and *adjusting*. **nroff** will use the unformatted text lines to create the formatted lines at the requested line length. Blank spaces are added between words to space out each line to fill the margins. The same poem will appear as

```
Mary  had  a  little  lamb.    Its  fleece  was
white  as  snow.  Everywhere  that  Mary  Went
The  lamb  was  sure  to  go.
```

Text that has straight right-hand margins, like the paragraph above, is said to be right-adjusted. **nroff** will right adjust the margin unless you specify otherwise. If you turn off the right justification, the paragraph will be formatted as the second example (with ragged right hand margin). Use the command

```
.na
```

to turn off the right justification feature. To turn right justification back on, use the **ad n** (adjust normal) command:

```
.ad n
```

Hyphenation and Line Adjustment Suppose that you had set the line width to 33 instead of 41. The result is shown below. **nroff** split the word "Everywhere" and printed it on two lines. When it's assembling a line, **nroff** tentatively adds each word to the line. If the new word makes the line longer than the allowed line length, **nroff** will

attempt to hyphenate the word. If the word can be hyphenated, as in the case of "Everywhere," the word will be split into two parts.

```
Mary had a little lamb.  Its
fleece was white as snow.  Every-
where that Mary Went The lamb was
sure to go.
```

The rules that **nroff** uses for hyphenating are simple. Occasionally, it will make the wrong decision. For example, if you reset the line length to 34, you get the following version of the nursery rhyme:

```
Mary had a little lamb.  Its flee-
ce was white as snow.  Everywhere
that Mary Went The lamb was sure
to go.
```

"Fleece" is not a word that you would ordinarily hyphenate. You can control hyphenation with the **hy** and **hn** commands. To turn hyphenation on, use

```
.hy
```

and use

```
.hn
```

to turn hyphenation off. Whether hyphenation is normally on or off seems to vary with the version of **nroff**. You may need to experiment to find out how your system is set up.

Paragraphs The **nroff** formatter can work with a number of different paragraph styles. A block paragraph is the simplest. In this form, all of the lines in the paragraph are left–aligned. The paragraph created with "Mary had a little lamb" is a block paragraph. An indented paragraph has the first line in the paragraph offset to the right. This paragraph is an indented paragraph. Hanging paragraphs are used in outlines and

lists. In this paragraph style, the first line will be flush left with the margin and all subsequent lines will be indented under the first line as in the following example:

> 1. Paragraph styles
>   a. Block
>   b. Indented
>   c. Hanging

Block Paragraphs One of the easiest ways to set off a section of text as a paragraph is to surround it with blank space. For example, let's format our nursery rhyme as two paragraphs—retaining the 41-character line length—by simply entering a blank line with the **sp** command.

```
.ll 41
Mary had a little lamb.
Its fleece was white as snow.
.sp
Everywhere that Mary Went
The lamb was sure to go.
```

nroff will produce the following two paragraphs in block format.

```
Mary had a little lamb.  Its fleece was
white as snow.

Everywhere that Mary Went The lamb was
sure to go.
```

You may not want blank lines to separate your paragraphs. In this case, use the **br** (break) command to stop the filling process as shown:

```
.ll 41
Mary had a little lamb.
Its fleece was white as snow.
```

```
.br
Everywhere that Mary Went
The lamb was sure to go.
```

and

```
Mary had a little lamb.   Its fleece was
white as snow.
Everywhere that Mary Went The lamb was
sure to go.
```

will be the result.

Indented Paragraphs To create an indented paragraph, simply offset the first line with blank spaces. Enter these either when you edit the document by inserting space manually or use the **ti** (temporary indent) command. This command will indent the following line by the specified number of blank spaces. For example,

```
.ll 41
.ti 5
Mary had a little lamb.
Its fleece was white as snow.
.sp
.ti 5
Everywhere that Mary Went
The lamb was sure to go.
```

will format the rhyme into the following two indented paragraphs:

```
     Mary had a little lamb.   Its fleece
was white as snow.

     Everywhere that Mary Went The
lamb was sure to go.
```

Hanging Paragraphs To format the poem in hanging paragraphs, offset all of the text by a specific amount and then move the first line to the left. To offset the text, use the **in** command. This command moves the text with respect to the left margin. The **in 10** command will offset all of the text by 10 spaces in our example. A positive number indicates the text is to be moved to the right. Then use the **ti -5** to move just the first line back to the left by 5 spaces

```
.ll 41
.in 10
.ti -5
Mary had a little lamb.
Its fleece was white as snow.
.sp
.ti -5
Everywhere that Mary Went
The lamb was sure to go.
```

and these commands turn the poem into the hanging paragraph below:

```
Mary had a little lamb.  Its fleece
     was white as snow.

Everywhere that Mary Went The
     lamb was sure to go.
```

This last technique is especially useful for generating outlines. To illustrate, let's turn "Mary" into an outline with these commands:

```
.ll 41
.nf
.in 10
.ti -5
A.  Mary had a little lamb.
1.  Its fleece was white as snow.
```

```
.sp
.ti -5
B.  Everywhere that Mary Went
1.  The lamb was sure to go.
```

This example, perhaps, shows more readily the use of hanging paragraphs. Note that you turned off the filling operation with the **nf** (no fill) command and the result is

```
A.  Mary had a little lamb.
    1.  Its fleece was white as snow.

B.  Everywhere that Mary Went
    1.  The lamb was sure to go.
```

Underlining There are two commands for underlining text: **ul** (underline) and **cu** (continuous underline). The **ul** command will underline only alphanumeric characters. The **cu** command will underline everything on the line—including blank spaces. Suppose you wish to underline the first line in the "Mary" outline. If you use the **ul** command

```
.ul
A.  Mary had a little lamb.
```

then command produces this underlining effect:

```
A.  Mary had a little lamb.
```

Note that neither the periods nor the blank spaces are underlined. To underline the entire line, periods, spaces and all, use the **cu** command:

```
.cu
A.  Mary had a little lamb.
```

and the command produces this underlining effect:

A. Mary had a little lamb.

You can specify that several consecutive lines are to be underlined by adding the number of lines to the command. For example, the **cu 5** command will underline the next five lines in your file. These are the lines in your document file, *not* the ones in your formatted document.

It's more likely that you will want to underline a particular word that an entire line. To underline a word, you must break up your line into two or more lines so that the word to be underlined is on a line by itself. To underline the word "little" in the first line of the rhyme, you place it on a separate line

```
Mary had a
.ul
little
lamb.
Its fleece ...
```

and the line will print as

> Mary had a <u>little</u> lamb.   Its ...

Overriding Justification When a line of text is right justified, extra blank spaces are added between the words. There may be situations where you will want to prevent extra blanks from being added between certain words. A name provides an excellent example. You will not want a name like R. A. Byers to be spaced out on a line

> . . . . . **R. A. Byers** . . . . .

Designating specific blanks to be treated like other characters for the purpose of justification will prevent extra spaces from being added. In **nroff**, back slashes placed in the text in front of the text in front of the spaces will identify these spaces. For example,

> . . . . . **R.\ A.\ Byers** . . . . .

will guarantee that the name will be formatted without additional blanks. The blank spaces after the back slashes are called *unpaddable* blanks.

Subscripts and Superscripts It may be necessary sometimes to print a *superscript*, a character printed slightly above the level of the other characters, or a *subscript*, a character slightly printed below the other characters. Both subscripts and superscripts are frequently used in mathematical equations and superscipts are often used to indicate footnotes or references.

nroff can identify characters as subscripts or superscripts. Using this capability requires that your printer can position up and down a half line. Many printers cannot do this. Ask your system administrator if your printer has this ability. If the system administrator isn't available, try it. Nothing bad will happen. At the worst, the characters will all be printed on the same line.

The **nroff** command for superscript (half line up) is **\u**. The command for a subscript (half line down) is **\d**. Unlike the other formatting codes discussed, these commands can be embedded in the text. They do *not* have to begin a line. Suppose you want to indicate a reference with superscript 2 in the following line:

```
...statement on American Politics2. He covered...
```

The line, including the formatting command, is entered as:

```
...statement on American Politics-u2-d. He covered...
```

Note that the **u** command is inserted before the superscript 2. This moves the line upward (toward the top of the paper). Then you enter all of the text to be printed at the new level: the character 2. The **d** command brings the printer back to the level of the rest of the line.

Tables Some of your documents may contain tables. You can enter tables by simply typing them in—using the space bar to align the columns—or you can use the tools that **nroff** provides for formatting tables. A table for a very small hardware store inventory is shown below:

PART NAME	QTY	PRICE
Hammer	6	10.88
Wrench, crescent	4	4.29
Pliers, gas	11	3.89

If your table is this small, it really doesn't matter too much how you enter it. In this book I can choose to work with small tables only, but you may not be so lucky. One important point to notice is that the number columns are aligned on their rightmost characters: They are *right–justified*. Don't forget to turn off justification and filling when entering tables—with the **na** and **nf** commands.

You can use the Tab key to help you layout the tables. The Tab key is much more powerful in **nroff** than it is on an ordinary typewriter. Usually, you set the tabs to begin at the leftmost position of a column. Then, you use the space bar to adjust your position within the column (if you are entering numbers). The tab control command is **ta**. This command sets the tabs to specified positions. The command

```
.ta 11,36,51
```

will set the tabs to the leftmost position of each of the three columns above. The data part of the inventory table would look like this:

```
.nf
.na
.ta 11,36,51
Hammer<TAB> 6<TAB>10.88
Wrench, crescent<TAB> 4<TAB> 4.29
Pliers, gas<TAB>11<TAB> 3.89
```

(<TAB> means press the Tab key). In **nroff**, you can specify both a tab type and a tab position. Specifying a tab position means that the following text should be right adjusted from that position or centered about that position. For the sample table, you can specify the right edge of the two number columns. The blank spaces inserted by

the Tab key are unpaddable blanks. They will *not* be affected if a line is justified. With the addition of **ta 11,37R,55R**, the edited text becomes:

```
.nf
.na
.ta 11,37R,55R
Hammer<TAB>6<TAB>10.88
Wrench, crescent<TAB>4<TAB>4.29
Pliers, gas<TAB>11<TAB>3.89
```

The difference between this version and the last is a subtle one. There are no blank spaces between the tabs and the following numbers. Instead, **nroff** takes care of adjusting the right edge of the two numeric columns.

Tables With Dotted Lines You may want to use tables that have dotted lines connecting two items separated on a page. A typical example is illustrated in the table below:

PART NAME	PRICE
Hammer	10.88
Wrench, crescent...	4.29
Pliers, gas	3.89

The dotted line helps the eye connect the separated items. Substitute ^A for the Tab key to use dotted lines instead of blank spaces in a table. That is, hold down the Control key while you press the "A" key. The editing process shows

```
.nf
.na
.ta 11,37R,55R
Hammer<^A>10.88
```

```
Wrench, crescent<^A>4.29
Pliers, gas<^A>3.89
```

APPENDIX 2

FOR THE

SYSTEM ADMINISTRATOR

Today's system administrator, who might be a manager, an engineer, a secretary, a lawyer, or even an accountant, usually has more responsibilities than just playing with the office computer. Because computers no longer always reside exclusively in a data processing department, they must be tended by someone working in the same physical area. This appendix is intended for the person who has been appointed as the system administrator and who is *not* a computer wizard.

In many cases, the system administrator is responsible for the routine operation and maintenance of the equipment, as well as handling catastrophes. You may be responsible for turning the computer on in the morning and off in evening. You will certainly be responsible for the administrative chores of assigning new users their login names, passwords, and group identifications—as well as helping acquaint them with the equipment and its procedures. You will also get the chore of removing users from the system.

In addition, you will most likely get to make backup copies of the disk files on floppy disks or whatever mechanism your computer has for storing data away from the computer. Similarly, you get to load files from floppies or tape into the computer. And, you will have the task of incorporating new equipment, such as additional memory, new terminals, and printers, into your system.

Turning the Computer On and Off

Turning the computer on may be as simple as flipping the "power on" switch and waiting for a few minutes, or it may require that you coax your computer to life one step at a time. What you have to do is dependent upon the vendor that supplied your

machine. Starting the computer is called *booting* it. This curious term comes from the phrase "lifting yourself up by your own bootstraps." The operating system is stored on the disk or on tape. The computer has to be told to read the operating system from the disk into memory. In most modern computers, a simple program stored in ROM will take care of this. When the computer starts itself upon power on, the process is called *autobooting*.

On an older machine, you might have to type in a series of commands to get everything started. If your computer does *not* autoboot, make sure that you have complete written instructions for coaxing it to life. Run through these instructions without any assistance before you let the vendor out the door. You will be amazed at how difficult things that seemed so obvious at the time the vendor was explaining them become, later, when you're trying to do them by yourself. Make certain you have a telephone number where you can call for help.

Many computers have a special file (usually written as a shell script) to help you bring the system up. This file is usually named "/etc/rc".

If you are starting your computer after some natural disaster such as a power failure or an accidental unplugging of the power cord, you had better run the command **fsck** (file system check). To run this utility program (command), you will need to know the device names of the disk drives on your computer. You should have these device names written down and you should keep the list in a safe place. The **fsck** command usually requires that you be logged in as the system administrator (root). The command will look something like

```
# fsck  /dev/idsk02 /dev/idsk05 /dev/idsk00
```

The items beginning with "/dev/" are the device names of the disks on your system. The "#" is the prompt assigned to the system administrator (root). The **fsck** command should correct minor problems with the file system. If it doesn't, call for help.

You should be aware that a sudden and inadvertent loss of power can cause damage to the file system. On some older computers, turning off the power without going through a shutdown procedure causes serious damage. On most modern systems, turning the power off simply initiates an automatic shutdown process. Be sure that you know which way to shut down your computer.

If you have better things to do with your time than cajole expensive hardware, you should make sure that the vendor has supplied you with shell programs to take care of start up and shutdown. This program is often named "shutdown."

The command, **sync**, is always included at the end of a "shutdown" program. This command is particularly important. It is used to ensure that all files are properly closed and put away before the power is actually removed from the system. UNIX folklore has it that you need to use this command several times. There seems to be substantial disagreement as to whether or not this is true. However, many manufacturers recommend that you do this and so, it's probably better to adhere to it than to be sorry. Failure to put the files to bed can damage the file structure and make your computer inoperable until the vendor or some other expert comes to repair it.

Adding New Users to the System

Another frequent task for the system administrator is adding new users to the system. On some of the newer systems, special programs are provided for this purpose. On AT&T's 3B2, for example, a menu program, **sysadm**, is used to take care of much of the day-to-day bother of being a system administrator. On this system, all the system administrator has to do is fill in a simple screen form for each new user. The menu program takes care of adding the new user information to the user file. It does so by using a program named **adduser**. **adduser**, or a similar program, may be found on many UNIX computer systems. The information that you will need to enter to add a new user to the system includes

> The new user's name
> Login name
> Identification number
> Group number
> Home directory name
> Password (optional)

This information will be stored in a file which is most often named "/etc/passwd". The data can either be entered via a program like **adduser** or it can be entered directly with

the **ed** or **vi** commands. The password file "/etc/passwd" is a simple text file that will look something like that shown in Figure 1.

```
allen:jRzE9zdHRD246:151:9:Allen Aardvark:/02/allen:
fff:ziMCvn9dYQRS6:152:11:Freddy Frog:/02/fff:
byers:NquKbocQDMFt1:157:9:Bob Byers:/02/byers:
```

Figure 1 Sample password file

This file is divided into fields (columns) that are separated by colons. Each of these columns contains specific information. The first column contains the user's login name. The second contains the password (the system codes the password). Next is the unique user identification number. The fourth column is the group identification number. The group number must be found in the file "/etc/group". The user's name follows and, finally, the user's home directory.

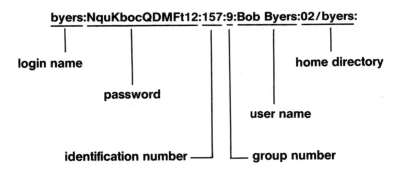

Figure 2 Field Assignments in the Password File

The login name is the name the user will use to log into the computer. The password is the encrypted version of the user's actual password. For example, the user password shown above is the encrypted version of the password "Robert". The identification number is a unique number that you assign to the user at the time he or she is added to the password file. The group number is used to indicate to the computer the primary group affiliation of the user. The user can belong to more than one group. The group listed in the password file is the group that the user will belong

FOR THE SYSTEM ADMINISTRATOR

to immediately upon login. The user name and the name of the home directory follows. If you are using a text editor to add a user to the system, add a line of text to the file "/etc/passwd". This line might look like

byers::157:9:Bob Byers:/02/byers:

Next, add the user's home directory to the system using the **mkdir** command. The example shows the command for creating the directory "/02/byers". You must be sure that the owner of the directory is the login name (or the user identification number). You can use the command **chown**:

$ chown byers /02/byers

or

$ chown 157 /02/byers

Finally, we want to give the user an initial password. Note that there is no password in our sample entry. To create the initial password, log into the system as the user and assign the initial password by using the **passwd** command. The user can select another password at a later time. While you are in the user's home directory, make a copy of the *standard user profile* file (.profile). This file will look something like the file shown as Figure 3. The file is usually named ".profile" and is stored in directory "/etc/".

```
$ cp /etc/profile   .profile
$ cat .profile
umask 7
stty erase ^H kill ^U echoe intr ^C
TERM=tvi950
export TERM
TZ=PST8PDT
export TZ
PATH=:/usr/local/bin:/usr/bin:/bin
export PATH
```

Figure 3 Sample user profile file .profile

This file's purpose is to set up the user's work area with specific instructions whenever the user logs in. (See the discussion in Chapter 2.) If you want to place special

restrictions on the user, you can incorporate those restrictions into the ".profile" file. To add a new user to your computer system:

1. Log in as the system administrator
2. Add the user to the password file
3. Create the user's home directory
4. Make the user the owner of the home directory
5. Log in as the user and assign an initial password

Removing Old Users from the System

To remove a user from the system, delete the line using the command **deluser** (if your system has this command). You can delete the line using either the **ed** or **vi** editors. To delete the user "byers" using the **vi** editor, type the command **vi /etc/passwd**. When the file comes on screen, move the cursor to the line containing the information for "byers." Press **dd** to delete the line and **:wq** to save the file with the changes intact.

Add a Group to the System

The groups are stored in the file "etc/group". Like the password file, this is an ordinary text file. Text files are often called ASCII files. The group file will look something like Figure 4.

```
root::0:root,bin,daemon
sys::3:root,adm,daemon
mail::4:root
project::9:fff
finance::11:
sales::15:tom,dick,harry,john,allen,\
edward,bill,bob
```

Figure 4 Sample group file

This file also uses colons to separate the fields. The first field contains the group name, the second contains the group password. In the sample file, none of the groups has a password. The third field contains the group number, and the last contains the login names of the users who belong to the group. The login names are separated by commas (*comma delimited*).

A user can be assigned to more than one group. For example, the user "root" (that's the system administrator) belongs to the groups "root," "sys," and "mail." The root must have the group number "0." The name must be "root" and there must be a password file entry for root. Even if you don't like the term, you must use it.

Note that the group "finance" has no users listed. You can omit the user list when it becomes extensive. UNIX uses the group number and not the user list. In "/etc/passwd" the group number is listed with each user's name. The user name list is for your convenience so that you can easily see who belongs to a group. When you do list the names, and the list is too long to fit on a single line you can use the backslash (\) to indicate that the line is continued. This is shown in the sales group in Figure 4.

Many systems will have a program, **addgroup,** to help you add a group to the group file. On the AT&T 3B2, this program is included with the many system utilities available with **sysadm.** On other systems, the **addgroup** program may exist as a stand-alone utility. In any case, you can add, change, and delete groups using the **ed** and **vi** editors.

Backing Up Disk Files

Most computer systems have some way of adding new software and backing up disk files with *removable media.* This term is a general one that covers tapes, disk cartridges, and floppy disks. Floppies are increasingly being used on systems that are intended for office or personal use. Tapes and disk cartridges are most often used on larger, professionally staffed installations. Some of the newer computers have features that simplify the process of copying files to and from removable media. For example, AT&T offers a host of easy-to-use utilities with its 3B2 office computer. These are referred to as *media-management commands.* They are available as individual commands or through the menu system offered by **sysadm.** These commands allow you to

APPENDIX 2

backup	Copy disk files to a floppy disk.
erase	Remove files from a floppy disk.
install	Copy disk files from a floppy disk.
restore	Copy files that had been backed up with backup from the backup floppy disk.
format	Format a floppy. Formatting a floppy disk prepares it for receiving data. This command requires that the system be in the single user mode—you have to kick all of the other users off the system. It is best to either purchase floppies that are already formatted or to format several floppies at one convenient time.

You can also copy your files to and from floppy disks using the command **cpio**. This command can also be used with certain magnetic tape drives if you know the device name of the floppy disk or the tape drive. The device names are located in the directory "/dev/". In the example command below, the name of the floppy disk is "/dev/flp". The procedure is

1. Select the directory with the **cd** command.
2. Place a floppy disk in the disk drive.
3. Copy the files from the selected directory with

```
$ ls | cpio -ocvB > /dev/flp
```

The command **cpio** offers numerous options. The options that we have demonstrated include

- **-o** This option outputs the listed files to the indicated ouput device. In the example, the output device is the floppy disk. If we had not *redirected* the output, the output would send all of the file contents to the screen.
- **-v** This option displays a list of the filenames that are copied.
- **-c** This option writes header information for each file copied.

-B This option sets the transfer rate from your system disk to the floppy disk. The data transfer rate is 5,120 bytes per second. The option is to be used only when the data is being copied to or from a floppy disk.

To restore the data from the floppy disk to your system disk use the **cpio** command with the **-i** (input) option:

```
$ cpio -icvB < /dev/flp
```

This is the "copy in" command. Note that the sample command uses the < to redirect the input to read the disk instead of the keyboard. There are, of course, many more options available with the **cpio** command. The illustrated options should cover the basic tasks of making and restoring backup copies of disk files.

On many larger systems the procedure to archive onto and retrieve from removable media is more formal. The user must become familiar with the three commands **mkfs**, **mount**, and **umount**. The **cpio** command copies your files to a floppy disk without making a directory on the floppy disk. Files copied in this way are intended as backups only. The **mkfs** program allows you to create a directory system on your floppy disk or on a removable cartridge disk.

When you create a directory system, you must tell **mkfs** how many disk blocks are to be allocated to the directory. The **mkfs** command is usually located in the "/etc/" directory. To use this command, select either the "/etc/" directory or specify its complete pathname. To illustrate the use of the **mkfs** command, let's make a directory system on our floppy disk. Assume the particular floppy disk will store up to three hundred sixty 1,024 byte blocks. To create the directory structure, insert a new floppy disk into the floppy disk drive and use the command

```
$ /etc/mkfs /dev/flp
```

To use this newly created disk file, you must create an empty directory (unless you already have one). Create a directory with the **mkdir** command. To create an empty directory named "floppydisk," you would use

```
$ mkdir floppydisk
```

Next, use the **mount** command, which, like **mkfs**, is usually located in the "/etc/" directory, to connect your floppy disk system to the new directory. Never use **mount** if the device you are mounting does not have a directory structure. The syntax or format of this command is given by:

```
mount device_to_be_mounted  directoryname
```

With the command

```
$ mount /dev/flp floppydisk
```

you can use this floppy disk just as though it were a permanent part of your directory system. You can copy files to and from this floppy disk with the **cp** command. You can execute programs that are stored on a floppy. You can actually do any operation that you would normally do with files that are a permanent part of your disk system. Floppy disks can often be used in this manner when the information they contain is confidential and needs to be kept more secure than information that is stored permanently on the main system disk drives.

When finished with your floppy, you must use the command **umount** (unmount). If you have moved into the floppy directory, you must first move back to the next higher directory. Then, you can **unmount** (disconnect) the device.

```
$ cd ..
$ umount /dev/flp
```

With this discussion, you have a brief summary of some of the more common tasks of the system administrator. On larger systems, the system administrator will have additional tasks to perform. On smaller systems, the system administrator may share these responsibilities with some of the other users. Remember, you can allocate or restrict access to any of the UNIX utility programs by using the **chmod** command to set the user access and assigning group access via the group file.

APPENDIX 3

ASCII CHART

CONTROL CHARACTERS

BINARY	HEX	DECIMAL	SYMBOL	CODE	DESCRIPTION
0000000	00	0	NUL	^@	Null
0000001	01	1	SOH	^A	Start of Heading
0000010	02	2	STX	^B	Start of Text
0000011	03	3	ETX	^C	End of Text
0000100	04	4	EOT	^D	End of Transmission
0000101	05	5	ENQ	^E	Enquiry
0000110	06	6	ACK	^F	Acknowledge
0000111	07	7	BEL	^G	Bell
0001000	08	8	BS	^H	Backspace
0001001	09	9	SH	^I	Horizontal Tabulation
0001010	0A	10	LF	^J	Line feed
0001011	0B	11	VT	^K	Vertical Tabulation
0001100	0C	12	FF	^L	Form feed
0001101	0D	13	CR	^M	Carriage Return
0001110	0E	14	SO	^N	Shift Out
0001111	0F	15	SI	^O	Shift In
0010000	10	16	DLE	^P	Data Link Escape
0010001	11	17	DC1	^Q	Device Control 1
0010010	12	18	DC2	^R	Device Control 2
0010011	13	19	DC3	^S	Device Control 3
0010100	14	20	DC4	^T	Device Control 4
0010101	15	21	NAK	^U	Negative Acknowledge
0010110	16	22	SYN	^V	Synchronous Idle
0010111	17	23	ETB	^W	End of Transmission Block
0011000	18	24	CAN	^X	Cancel
0011001	19	25	EM	^Y	End of Medium
0011010	1A	26	SUB	^Z	Substitute
0011011	1B	27	ESC	^[	Escape
0011100	1C	28	FS	^\	File Separator
0011101	1D	29	GS	^]	Group Separator
0011110	1E	30	RS	^^	Record Separator
0011111	1F	31	US	^_	Unit Separator
1111111	7F	127	DEL	DEL	Delete

APPENDIX 3

PRINTABLE CHARACTERS

BINARY	HEX	DECIMAL	SYMBOL	BINARY	HEX	DECIMAL	SYMBOL
0100000	20	32	SPACE	1010000	50	80	P
0100001	21	33	!	1010001	51	81	Q
0100010	22	34	"	1010010	52	82	R
0100011	23	35	#	1010011	53	83	S
0100100	24	36	$	1010100	54	84	T
0100101	25	37	%	1010101	55	85	U
0100110	26	38	&	1010110	56	86	V
0100111	27	39	'	1010111	57	87	W
0101000	28	40	(	1011000	58	88	X
0101001	29	41	)	1011001	59	89	Y
0101010	2A	42	*	1011010	5A	90	Z
0101011	2B	43	+	1011011	5B	91	[
0101100	2C	44	,	1011100	5C	92	\
0101101	2D	45	−	1011101	5D	93	]
0101110	2E	46	.	1011110	5E	94	^
0101111	2F	47	/	1011111	5F	95	_
0110000	30	48	0	1100000	60	96	`
0110001	31	49	1	1100001	61	97	a
0110010	32	50	2	1100010	62	98	b
0110011	33	51	3	1100011	63	99	c
0110100	34	52	4	1100100	64	100	d
0110101	35	53	5	1100101	65	101	e
0110110	36	54	6	1100110	66	102	f
0110111	37	55	7	1100111	67	103	g
0111000	38	56	8	1101000	68	104	h
0111001	39	57	9	1101001	69	105	i
0111010	3A	58	:	1101010	6A	106	j
0111011	3B	59	;	1101011	6B	107	k
0111100	3C	60	<	1101100	6C	108	l
0111101	3D	61	=	1101101	6D	109	m
0111110	3E	62	>	1101110	6E	110	n
0111111	3F	63	?	1101111	6F	111	o
1000000	40	64	@	1110000	70	112	p
1000001	41	65	A	1110001	71	113	q
1000010	42	66	B	1110010	72	114	r
1000011	43	67	C	1110011	73	115	s
1000100	44	68	D	1110100	74	116	t
1000101	45	69	E	1110101	75	117	u
1000110	46	70	F	1110110	76	118	v
1000111	47	71	G	1110111	77	119	w
1001000	48	72	H	1111000	78	120	x
1001001	49	73	I	1111001	79	121	y
1001010	4A	74	J	1111010	7A	122	z
1001011	4B	75	K	1111011	7B	123	{
1001100	4C	76	L	1111100	7C	124		
1001101	4D	77	M	1111101	7D	125	}
1001110	4E	78	N	1111110	7E	126	~
1001111	4F	79	O	1111111	7F	127	DEL

GLOSSARY

ACCESS PERMISSIONS

Codes that determine who may use a particular file and how each user may use the file. The possible access permissions are "read," "write," and "execute."

ARGUMENT

The part of the command line that specifies what the command is to do.

ASCII ORDER

The order in which letters, numbers, and special symbols appear according to the "American Standard Code for Information Interchange." See Appendix 3.

AUTOBOOT

The process by which a computer is brought automatically to its operating configuration upon application of power.

BACKGROUND PROCESS

A process which runs behind the active process appearing on the computer terminal.

BACKUP

A copy of programs or data made as insurance against loss of data from possible computer failure.

BATCH PROCESSING

Where a series of programs or data processing tasks are executed one at a time.

BIT

Binary Digit. The basic processing unit of a computer. A bit can be set to a "1" or a "0."

BOOT

The process of starting the computer, that is, loading the operating system.

BOOT PROGRAM

A program used to "bootstrap" the computer into loading the operating system.

BOURNE SHELL

A program used to interface the computer to the interactive user. The Bourne shell is the shell program most often used with AT&T versions of UNIX.

BUFFER

A temporary storage area.

BYTE

The amount of memory used to store a character such as an "A." A byte consists of eight bits.

C PROGRAMMING LANGUAGE

A computer language that is midway between traditional high-level languages and assembly language.

CENTRAL PROCESSING UNIT

The part of the computer that actually does the computing.

CHARACTER

A printable symbol, such as "A" or "," or "3".

CHARACTER PRINTER

A printer that prints one character at a time.

CHARACTER STRING

A sequence of characters. The sequence may contain blank spaces. The sequence "10150 W. Jefferson Blvd." is a character string.

COMMAND

A sequence of words and/or symbols that instruct the computer to perform a specific task.

COMMAND INTERPRETER

The process that "reads" the commands and translates them into language the computer understands.

COMPARE

The process of comparing two files or two character strings.

CONTROL KEY

A key that is used in the same manner as the shift key to impart a third meaning to letter keys on the terminal keyboard.

CONTROL CHARACTER

A letter character used in conjunction with the Control key to provide special command information to the computer. For example, ^D is used in UNIX to signal the end of a process.

CURSOR

A visible marker that indicates the present position of the CRT's electron beam on the screen. It usually takes the form of a blinking square.

DEFAULT

The action the computer is to take if no further information is provided. An assumed value or instruction.

DELIMIT

To mark or set off. For example, character strings are often set off by double quotes ("). The symbols, such as quotation marks, are called delimiters.

DICTIONARY ORDER

An alternative to ASCII order. In dictionary order the characters are arranged with special symbols first, then numbers, then letters.

DISK DIRECTORY

A disk file containing the names and disk locations of other disk files.

DISK FILES

Groups of information or programs stored on a disk under a single file name.

EDITOR

A program to edit the contents of text or document files.

EOF

End of File. In UNIX, the end-of-file marker is usually a ^D .

EOT

End of Transmission. This marker is used to indicate the end of a communications sequence, such as in the **write** command.

ESCAPE

A special control character (^[) used to control the operation of printers and terminals.

EXECUTE

To run a program.

FIELD

A column in a table of rows and columns.

FIELD SEPARATOR

The symbol used to indicate column (field) boundaries for use in sort and other UNIX commands.

FILE OWNER

The creator of a disk file.

FILE EXTENSION

A group of characters affixed to the end of a disk filename by an applications program. File extensions usually consist of a period and three characters.

FILENAME

The name assigned to a disk file. Filenames can consist of up to 14 letters and numbers.

FILTER

A process to transform the contents of a file.

FOREGROUND PROCESS

The operation going on in the computer's foreground. This is the process that is visible on the computer terminal.

FORMATTER

A program that gives form to the displayed output of a program.

GLOBAL

Pertaining to an entire group. All characters in a file, or all files in a directory.

GROUP

One or more computer users that have been identified to the computer as belonging to the same unit.

GROUP ID

An identification number assigned to members of the group.

HOME DIRECTORY

The working directory of a user immediately upon logging in.

INPUT/OUTPUT

The computer circuits and software associated with getting data into the computer and with outputting it to peripheral devices such as printers, terminals, and disk drives.

INTERACTIVE

A computer process that sets up a dialogue between the computer and the user.

INTERPRETER

A computer program that translates English-like commands into machine commands.

INVISIBLE FILENAMES

Filenames that have a period for their opening character. For example, .profile is an invisible filename. Invisible filenames are not displayed with the ordinary **ls** command.

KERNEL

The core of UNIX. This is the part of UNIX that actually controls the computer hardware and that acts as an interface between the computer and computer programs.

KILL

To stop or terminate a command or process.

LINE EDITOR

An editor that deals with a single line of text at a time.

LINE PRINTER

A printer that prints an entire line of text at a time.

LINK

To attach an alternative name to a file. To hook one process to another.

LOGIN

To identify yourself as a proper user to the computer.

LOGIN NAME

An identifying code used to gain access to the computer.

LOGOUT

To formally exit from the computer's environment.

MAIL

A program or set of programs that allow users to send electronic messages to each other.

MAIN MEMORY

The electronic memory that is directly accessible by the Central Processing Unit.

MEDIA-MANAGEMENT COMMANDS

A set of commands that are provided to help manage the disk resources of the computer.

METACHARACTER

Special characters that are used to help define classes of symbols or groups of symbols. The most common metacharacters are the "?", " *", and "[ ]".

MODEM

A device for connecting the user's terminal to the computer over a telephone line. MODEM is an acronym for MOdulator-DEModulator.

MULTI-USER

A multi-user operating system is capable of supporting more than one user at the same time.

MULTI-TASKING

Multi-tasking means that the operating system is capable of allowing more than one user to use the same program at the same time or allowing one user to perform more than one task at a time.

OFF LINE

Equipment that can be, but is not currently, directly connected to the computer.

ON LINE

Equipment that is currently electrically connected and directly accessible to the computer system.

OPERATING SYSTEM

The software system used to control the computer hardware.

OPTION

An available special feature of a command.

OWNER

The creator of a disk file.

PASSWORD

A secret word or character sequence used to gain admittance to the computer system.

PATH

A route tracing from the root (main) directory to the file of interest.

PATHNAMES

The *absolute* pathname is the complete filename, consisting of the filename and all directory names between the file and the root directory. The *relative* pathname is the name of the file and all directory names between the file and the user's working directory.

PIPE

A process of connecting commands so that the output of one command is automatically the input to the succeeding command.

PIPING

The sequence of commands forming a pipe.

PORTABILITY

The capability to move software and data files to other computer systems.

GLOSSARY

POSITIONAL VARIABLES

The mapping of an argument in a command to a variable that matches the position of the argument in sequence.

PRINT OPTIONS

Choices available when printing a file.

PRIVATE

A file which is reserved for the private use of an individual user.

PROCESS

The operation initiated by a command. For example, the sort command initiates the sorting process.

PROMPT

The symbol used to indicate that the system is ready to accept a command or instruction. The normal UNIX prompt is the $ (dollar sign).

PROTECTION

Preventing accidental erasure or alteration of a disk file. You protect a file by setting the read/write permissions to "read only."

PUBLIC

A file or program which is available to all system users.

RANDOM ACCESS MEMORY (RAM)

The part of the computer's main memory that can be loaded and changed. Random access also means that the memory is directly addressable.

READ

This is the ability to display or print the contents of a file.

READ ONLY MEMORY (ROM)

The part of the computer's memory that cannot be changed. This type of memory is usually reserved for special functions, including "booting."

REDIRECTION

The routing of the output of a command to a destination other than its standard (or default) destination.

REGULAR EXPRESSION

A general class or pattern found in character strings.

REMOVABLE MEDIA

Floppy disks, tapes, and removable hard disk cartridges are called removable media because they can be removed from the computer.

ROOT DIRECTORY

The main, or top, directory in a computer system.

SCREEN EDITOR

An editor that takes advantage of the characteristics of the video terminal to perform editing.

SEARCH

The process of having the computer hunt for a particular pattern or character string in a file or group of files. Also, the process of searching the directory for a filename.

SHELL

The part of the operating system that interacts with the user. In UNIX, the shell is a program that provides the connection between the user and the operating system.

SHELL COMMANDS

These are commands that are unique to a particular shell. They are included to provide the user the capability to customize commands and to create special commands for convenience.

SHELL SCRIPT

A program written using the shell commands.

SORT

The process of rearranging the contents of a file so that they appear in alphabetical, chronological, or numeric order.

SPOOLING

The process for queuing print tasks in a computer. As a job is sent to the printer, it is placed in a queue until the printer is available.

STANDARD INPUT

The keyboard is the standard input for most UNIX commands.

STANDARD OUTPUT

The terminal screen is the standard output for most UNIX commands.

STANDARD USER PROFILE

A program that is set up in each user home directory which defines the normal working environment for the user. The profile is stored in the shell script ".profile".

STRING

Same as a character string.

SUBDIRECTORY

A directory that belongs to another directory.

SYSTEM ADMINISTRATOR

The user who is responsible for the day-to-day operations of the computer system.

SYSTEM CLOCK

A device that sends signals to the computer which are interpreted as time and date.

TEES

A method for sending the standard output of a command to two locations at once. For example, a **tee** can route the output of a command to both a disk file and the terminal screen.

UTILITY PROGRAM

A general purpose program. The commands in UNIX are each separate utility programs. When you use the command **cat**, you are calling up the UNIX utility program with that name.

VARIABLE

A temporary storage area.

WILDCARD

A symbol that can be substituted for classes of characters. The ".", "?", " *", and "[ ]" are the most common wildcards.

WRITE

Permission to create, change, or erase a disk file. Also the name of a UNIX command to communicate with other users of the computer.

Index

SURVEY

Thank you for purchasing an Ashton-Tate book.
Our readers are important to us. Please take a few moments to provide us with some information, so we can better serve you.

Name: _____

Company Name: _____

Address: _____

City/State: _____ Zip: _____

Country: _____ Date: _____

1) How did you first learn about this publication?
21-1 ( ) Someone who saw or bought it
-2 ( ) Software dealer or salesperson
-3 ( ) Hardware dealer or salesperson
-4 ( ) Advertising
-5 ( ) Published review
-6 ( ) Computer store display
-7 ( ) Computer show
-8 ( ) Book store
-9 ( ) Directly from Ashton-Tate

2) Where did you purchase this publication?
22-1 ( ) Directly from Ashton-Tate™
-2 ( ) From my dBASE II® Dealer
-3 ( ) Computer show
-4 ( ) Book store

3) Have you purchased other Ashton-Tate books and publications?
23-1 ( ) Yes 23-2 ( ) No
If Yes, please check which ones:
23-3 ( ) *dBASE II for the First-Time User*
-4 ( ) *Data Management for Professionals*
-5 ( ) *System Design Guide*
-6 ( ) *dNEWS™*
-7 ( ) *Through the MicroMaze*
-8 ( ) *Everyman's Database Primer*
-9 ( ) *Reference Encyclopedia for the IBM® Personal Computer*
-10 ( ) *IBM PC Public Domain Software, Vol. I*

4) What type of software programs are you using now?
24-1 ( ) Accounting
-2 ( ) Spreadsheet
-3 ( ) Word Processing
-4 ( ) Other (Please specify) _____
_____

5) What type of software programs are you interested in?
25-1 ( ) Academic/Scientific
-2 ( ) Agriculture
-3 ( ) Building
-4 ( ) Business
-5 ( ) Financial
-6 ( ) Health Care
-7 ( ) Home/Hobby
-8 ( ) Insurance
-9 ( ) Membership/Registry
-10 ( ) Professional
-11 ( ) Real Property
-12 ( ) Software Utilities
-13 ( ) Spreadsheet
-14 ( ) Integrated

6) Whom are you purchasing the book for?
27-1 ( ) Business
-2 ( ) Self

7a) Who will be the actual reader?
28-1 ( ) I will be
-2 ( ) Someone else will be
Title: _____

7b) What make and model computer do you use?
28-3 _____

8) Do you expect to purchase other software programs during the next 12 months? If so, what type?
29-1 ( ) Accounting
-2 ( ) Sales
-3 ( ) Inventory
-4 ( ) Other (Please specify)_____
_____

9) What subjects would you like to see discussed?
30-1 _____
_____
_____

10) How can we improve this book?
31-1 _____
_____
_____

11) What is your primary business?
A. Computer Industry
32-1 ( ) Manufacturing
-2 ( ) Systems house
-3 ( ) DP supply house
-4 ( ) Software
-5 ( ) Retailing
-6 ( ) Other
B. Non-Computer Business
33-1 ( ) Manufacturing
-2 ( ) Retail trade
-3 ( ) Wholesale trade
-4 ( ) Financial, banking
-5 ( ) Real estate, insurance
-6 ( ) Engineering
-7 ( ) Government
-8 ( ) Education

34-1 ( ) Military
-2 ( ) Health services
-3 ( ) Legal services
-4 ( ) Transportation
-5 ( ) Utilities
-6 ( ) Communications
-7 ( ) Arts, music, film
-8 ( ) Other _____

12) What is your position and title? Please check one in each list
POSITION
35-1 ( ) Data processing
-2 ( ) Engineering
-3 ( ) Marketing/Advertising
-4 ( ) Sales
-5 ( ) Financial
-6 ( ) Legal
-7 ( ) Administration
-8 ( ) Research
-9 ( ) Operations/production
-10 ( ) Distribution
-11 ( ) Education
-12 ( ) Other _____
TITLE
35-13 ( ) Owner
-14 ( ) Chairperson
-15 ( ) President
-16 ( ) Vice President
-17 ( ) Director
-18 ( ) Manager
-19 ( ) Dept. head
-20 ( ) Independent contractor
-21 ( ) Scientist
-22 ( ) Programmer
-23 ( ) Assistant
-24 ( ) Other _____

13) How many employees are in your company?
36-1 ( ) Less than 10
-2 ( ) 10 to 25
-3 ( ) 26 to 100
-4 ( ) 101 to 300
-5 ( ) 301 to 1,000
-6 ( ) over 1,000

14) I would like to remain on your mailing list.
37-1 ( ) Yes 37-2 ( ) No

38-1 I'd like to purchase additional copies of the current edition of this book at $17.95 plus $1.50 handling.
☐ My check is enclosed
My MasterCard/Visa card number is:

_____

Expiration date _____

Signature _____

©1985, Ashton-Tate

ASHTON·TATE ™

10150 WEST JEFFERSON BOULEVARD
CULVER CITY, CALIFORNIA 90230